FALLEN LEAVES

FALLEN LEAVES

LIFE, DEATH, AND THE SEASONS BETWEEN

A MEMOIR

JEAN STARLING

STARLING

ISBN: 979-8-9933872-3-9

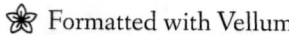 Formatted with Vellum

Dedication

I dedicate this book to my family

Roman Starling

Born: August 18, 1920, Died: March 24, 1954, age 33

Flossie Irene Jackson Starling

Born October 2, 1922, Died: July 15, 1990, age 67

Berline: *Born: June 17, 1950, Died: August 15, 1991, age 41*

Bertha: *Born: September 10, 1943, Died: March 24, 1995, age 52*

Carol: *Born: June 26, 1945, Died: May 5, 1995, age 50*

Roman Jr: *Born: April 20, 1940, Died: April 15, 1998, age 58*

Ruth: *Born: March 2, 1948, Died: September 18, 2005, age 56*

Gaston: *Born: November 18, 1941, Died: June 22, 2011, age 69*

Roma: *Born: September 03, 1954, Died: January 08, 2019, age 65*

James: *Born: January 20, 1953*

Feelings Buried Alive
Never Die

CONTENTS

Introduction   xi

Chapter 1   1
The First Leaf Falls

Chapter 2   17
The Wolves Come Out

Chapter 3   33
Mama's Life Without Daddy

Chapter 4   53
My Life as A Teen Bride

Chapter 5   66
The South Calls Me Home

Chapter 6   71
Daddy's Face on my Twin

Chapter 7   75
Death Comes for My Mama

Chapter 8   90
Half of me Missing

Chapter 9   117
The Special Sister

Chapter 10   127
The Contagious Laugh

Chapter 11   138
The Patriarch Dies

Chapter 12   147
Ruth's Winter

Chapter 13   158
On Her Terms

Chapter 14   185
We Are the Message

Epilogue   200

Appendix   203

About the Author   217

INTRODUCTION

In my mind's eye, I'm walking down the dirt road that winds around our farm in North Carolina. Sunlight filters through the bright pink dogwood trees and their blossoms overhead. Honeysuckle vines that grow on the side of the road release their sweet smell into the warm southern air, their perfume lulling me into a peaceful reverie.

On that day, it was easy to believe in an all-knowing, all-powerful God who saw me, loved me, and kept watch over our family. But that peace didn't last. My path soon grew jagged, and my pain felt like a cold, relentless rain chilling me to the bone. I found myself asking questions I wasn't sure there was an answer to: *Why us? Does God really care about me and my family?* Still, I pressed onward. Self-preservation became a powerful motivator, because I knew that if I gave up, the burden would crush me.

My coping strategy was simple: I pushed my feelings as far down as they would go, set aside for later, perhaps never. Life is always busy, and it was easy enough to convince myself there would be time *later* to deal with things, though later never seemed to come.

Our world changed forever when my daddy, Roman, died at only thirty-three, leaving Mama with eight children and another on the way. I was almost four—old enough to feel the shift, too young to understand it.

Seasons came and went—humid southern summers giving way to the golden leaves of fall. With each passing season, our family endured more than our share of life's cold, relentless rain. Disease, death, molestation, abuse, violence—our family would come to know them all.

Just as the golden leaves of a great oak turn brown and fall one by one, so too have the members of my family slipped away. Each time Death roared through our lives, I shoved the pain deeper and tried to outrun the trauma. I learned that grief arrives in seasons—some fierce like the winds that strip the trees bare, others gentle like the last golden leaf clinging stubbornly to its branch. Each loss carried its own color, shape, and place in the tapestry of my life.

When I finally understood that *feelings buried alive never die*, I began writing about my family—not only to honor their memories and celebrate their lives, but also to pour out the fear, anger, and grief I had carried for so long. I didn't have a particular agenda when I began; I simply allowed my spirit to guide my hands. Before long, the story took on a life of its own. I was only the conduit. Whatever the reason, our story demanded to be written.

This writing became an excavation of our shared history, exposing painful truths about my parents, my siblings, and myself. It is a testament to the courage of the human spirit to push onward despite everything.

Fallen Leaves is a story of connection, written with the hope that anyone enduring cruelty, grief, or the haunting question *"Why me?"* might find comfort and support within these pages. Death and disease, abuse and violence—no one should have to suffer alone. By sharing our sometimes-rugged road of life, I hope we can help shoulder the weight of the burdens that threaten to crush us. I'm grateful we're walking this path together.

This is a story of love, loss, and the quiet beauty of remembrance.

The First Leaf Falls...

CHAPTER 1
THE FIRST LEAF FALLS

Ten dirt-poor Southerners, pecking out a living growing tobacco in the deep blue South.

The Daddy died, without him by their side nine little Southerners hungry in the South.

The Mama's last little baby girl was born, so now she had nine, nine little Southern barefoot kids, pecking out a living growing tobacco in the deep blue South.

Fighting and crying, hugging and loving, scrambling to survive; head bent, mama sighing, ten little Southerners living in the South.

Got big they did; those little Southern boys and girls grew into men and women pecking out a living in the deep blue South.

Some moved away, some stayed put, all shoved their fears deep inside trying to hide from the remaining crew; deep blue pain the Southern winds blew.

Next went the Mama to be with the Daddy. Now there were nine little Southerners left to live.

Following the Mama Death came to call; took one of the twins away from us all. Eight little Southerners left to live.

Now the eldest sister left to be with the lord. Older but not old, she still had to go. Seven little southerners left to live.

Only a few weeks till Death called, let's take the sister next in this clan of little Southerners pecking out a living in the deep blue South. Six little southerners left to live.

Death satisfied took leave from the Southerners that soggy fall. Gave them a little reprieve to prepare for his next call.

Summers blaze smolders hot time for the patriarch of this lot. Took the eldest brother and now that just left two brothers in this little Southern crew. Five little Southerners left to live.

The Death Angel gazed with pity on the little Southern clan, said, You know, I think I'll give them a while in the sun and Southern sand, to heal!

Six years pacing at the gate No more time to wait. Now's the season for the middle red-headed Southern girl; four little Southerners left to live.

Watching behind the curtain yonder Leaves us to ponder when will his death rattle win the battle till no more little Southerners left to live!

I t all started with Daddy's death.

I'm not sure how to share this story of my family's deaths, or how to tell you about the long, painful dying that came before. The writing of this story has found me, rather than me it, so I have made the decision to begin and allow it to unfold as it will.

Many of my family members have died, and the death process was a long and painful living death for them. Sometimes the pain of their dying process and then their death is all I can feel. It is only as I shut down some part of my spirit that I can forget and continue to live my daily life with all its duties. Their deaths, their lives, and my life as it relates to them are what I write about.

Over the past year or so it has become clear to me that I cannot continue to hide away a part of me inside, so I'm hoping in some way to heal as I write this book. I'm also hoping that reading about the pain, fear, and survival that is a part of my innermost being will help someone else heal their own pain.

Pain of dying
pain of death
pain of living

> pain of loss
> pain of not being totally real
> pain of hiding away inside
> so that I might survive.

I was born and grew up in the South—farmland North Carolina to be exact. "Grew up" is a relative term as I got married at age fourteen and left the South; little did I know it then, but there was a whole lot more growing up to do. I have come to term it "our South" as I'm sure that for many others "their South" was much different than ours, but our South is the only one I know so our South with all the good, the bad and the in between is what I write about.

We lived and worked on a farm growing tobacco and water-melons as our main crops. I loved seeing the watermelons ripening on the vines, growing bigger each day, almost like a woman pregnant with her child. Then when they come to full term, the baby is born with all sweetness and life. Like the heart of the melon, so pure and fresh, and it being the best part with its big, red, luscious center. Daddy used mules to pull the harrow to plow the fields. It was back breaking work to harvest the crops in those days.

Mama always had a garden filled with butter beans, watermelons, yellow long crooked squash, snap peas, okra, collard greens and corn. We had fat back and collard greens, boiled potatoes, and fried corn bread or homemade biscuits for many of our meals. For breakfast we either had grits, which to me tasted grainy and slimy, with one or two eggs cooked in a big pot so that you got mostly grits with a touch of egg. Or we might have fritters, which was merely flour and water mixed up, fried, and served with dark molasses syrup poured over the top. A family favorite was to put homemade biscuits broken into small chunks into a cup, sprinkle them with sugar and then pour coffee over the top. I've never found anything to taste quite this good. Dinner, which was a midday meal and our biggest meal of the day, we invariably had biscuits and potatoes, collard greens, fat back, and maybe some peas or butter beans; our evening meal was called supper.

There wasn't much in the way of store-bought food. As farmers we grew most of what we ate. We didn't have the money to spend on candy and snacks from the store and even if we had, Mama and Daddy would have thought spending money on them would have been wasteful. As kids we wanted food from the store, but I sure would give anything to be able to go back and have one of Mama's home cooked meals today.

All our roads were dirt back then, so we were always barefoot. I cannot even remember wearing shoes much at all those first few years, but I do remember walking in the sand and it is coming up through my toes.

Even though I cannot really remember seeing very many snakes, I grew up with a morbid fear of them that continues to this day. I know that being out on the farm we must have had snakes all around us in the fields; there was always a lot of storytelling about snakes that got into houses and on top of people. I can't count the nightmares I've had about snakes getting in and on top of me—way too many.

While the summers were long and hot and the air filled with the smells of tobacco and watermelons, the winters were spent indoors, around our little wood stove in the kitchen. It didn't seem like the winters were very long or very cold, though. I don't really remember even owning a coat as a little kid.

Occasionally now I sit daydreaming, allowing my mind to drift back to our farm. I remember one tree that stood by the shed in our yard. That was the climbing tree for us kids. My sisters and brothers would climb up on the shed, jump over to the tree limb and then jump down, so if I didn't want to be called a scaredy-cat, of course I had to jump as well. By the time I reached the top of the shed my hands would be clammy with fear. To this day, my stomach still knots with apprehension at the thought of that tree.

We didn't have much in the way of toys as kids, but then we didn't seem to need them. We made up our own games to play. One fun game involved tying old tobacco strings to the feet of fireflies, lightning bugs we called them, and then running around with the bugs flying and us chasing after them, hanging onto the strings. The bugs had a light on their heads, so they looked like they had headlights.

Another fun game we played was 'doodlebug doodlebug' with little black bugs, which I think are a type of potato bug that lives in the ground. We'd take a little stick or blade of grass and poke it into the top of the sand hill and move it around with a circular motion, all the while singing this little song to get the bugs to come out. We called them doodlebugs because they made squiggly lines in the sand.

Doodlebug
Doodlebug
Come out tonight
Your house is on fire
Your cornbread is in the oven
Doodlebug doodlebug
Come out tonight

It was always such an amazing thing to see those bugs come wriggling out. We didn't know that we were too poor to afford toys; we had so much fun with our made-up games, we just assumed this was what all kids did.

We slept four and five to a bed back then, and I remember dreaming of having to go to the bathroom, which for us at the time was an outdoor toilet. After wetting the bed, I'd awaken, heart pounding, to find myself and my brothers and sisters wet from my puddle. I can still feel the shame of those nights when I would jump up and change my underwear so the other kids wouldn't know it was me who had wet the bed where we lay.

I was about four years old when Daddy died (March 24, 1954). I can't seem to remember much about him no matter how hard I try. I just realized that I have always thought of him as Daddy, not Dad. I guess it's because he died when I was so young; for me he will always be Daddy. You have a certain relationship with your daddy when you are a child, and then if you're one of the fortunate ones, you have an adult relationship with him. We never had the opportunity for our relationship to grow into more than a little girl and her daddy.

The only thing I seem to be able to remember about my Daddy is his face as he lay dead in that dark blue coffin with the white satin lining, the coffin resting up against the wall in our living room. I can still see the coffin against the wall and him lying in it. His face looked so handsome and so strong, how could he be gone? What haunts me most is that I cannot remember anything about him holding me or playing with me. Why must it be that the only thing I remember of him is him lying there in that coffin?

Today, I know he was sick for a long time before he died and that he "lost his mind," as the saying went in the South. All throughout my childhood years there were various little pieces of information that came out, stories told and retold. Daddy was a farmer with eight kids to support and a farm to run—a hard worker.

From what I understand, he had a mental breakdown, which, given the circumstances wasn't so unusual. His life would have been filled with tiredness, aches and pains that must have accompanied his every move from the stress of raising a large family and finding ways to support them. Today I'm sure he'd be prescribed an antidepressant and hopefully get some rest; then he'd be fine. At the time, Mama put him in a hospital for treatment. My grandparents wanted her to keep him at home, locked in an outbuilding where he couldn't hurt himself or us. What truly amazes me is that as horrible as the idea is that he'd have been locked in a little outbuilding at home, he might have lived had Mama done so. Instead, he was taken seventy miles away to a private mental facility in Chapel Hill, North Carolina.

To understand what they did to Daddy, I had to learn about the "treatments" of that time. In 1954, the treatment for mental illness and depression was Electroconvulsive (ECT) Therapy and Insulin Coma Therapy (ICT), which was an insulin-induced coma. After the treatment, glucose was administered to bring the person out of the coma. Daddy wouldn't have had a choice in this treatment because they didn't require prior consent, and even if they had, I'm sure Mama and Daddy wouldn't have understood the risks associated with it.

ECT involves the use of controlled electrical currents of one to two seconds in duration that induce a 30-second seizure. Generally, the procedure involves attaching two electrodes to the scalp, one on each side of the head, although physicians sometimes place the electrodes on only one side of the head. Often, two or three treatments are given weekly for several weeks. In its early years, ECT was administered to patients without prior medication. (Fink, 1999)

These treatments caused a lack of memory for both the simplest of activities and for those people who you knew and loved before.

Daddy spent about eight months in that facility, where they consistently gave him electroshock therapy and insulin-induced coma shock therapy. After a time, he was able to come home on the weekends to see us kids and Mama. It was on his last weekend home before he died that Mama conceived my youngest sister, Roma. Now Mama had eight kids and one more on the way to worry about.

Years later, when my sister Roma was older, Mama told her some things about that time. She questioned her own decision to put Daddy in the hospital, but at the time, she just didn't know what else to do. She couldn't understand why, when he came home, Daddy couldn't remember her, or us, or how to farm the land. So not understanding that the method of treatment they were giving him was causing his loss of memory, he kept going back.

Mama said that while he was home, Daddy would pray for God to give him strength to go back without a fight. It rips me apart inside to think of him being put through shock therapy, losing his memory and not understanding why, and then praying that he could continue so that he could be made well again. Obviously, that didn't happen.

When Mama was finally out of money, she sent him to the state mental institution, Dorthea Dix Hospital, where they told her that Daddy had been given too many shock treatments. Their remedy was to use the insulin-induced coma treatment and then use glucose to bring him back out of the coma. One morning, when they gave him the insulin, he had a massive heart attack and died. I wonder how many other daddies, mamas, and children died from this inhumane "treatment."

At any rate, Daddy died in the hospital, and I can only imagine how horrible his death must have been. I can't let myself dwell on it too much though, because it makes me feel as if my chest will cave in. His death certificate merely states that he died of heart failure, but it conveniently omits the fact that the heart failure was caused by too many insulin and shock treatments.

Sadly, we'll never know how long my Daddy might have lived if he hadn't been subjected to this medical experimentation, but because of it, his death always remained a black thing in our lives, always something not understood, and always questioned.

Mama did try to get information from the hospital and from the doctors, but to no avail. She obviously passed her suspicions on to us, because we always assumed there was something amiss in Daddy's death. Years later, when my twin sister Berline was in nursing school, she went to the hospital and saw the records. That's when she learned the truth. It was only when I began writing this book that I learned the truth as well. My fears and hiding from hurt always kept me from asking the questions until now. The hospital had given him too much insulin and because of it, the nine of us had grown up without a father.

I never checked the records and sometimes I wonder why. I believe I did not want to know, did not want to be sure; maybe to have suspicions about the cause of his death was better than to know for sure. To know for sure that so much pain in our lives was caused by the doctors' and hospitals' experimentation.

Doctors who did not fully understand the consequences of electroshock treatment and insulin treatments for depression had used my Daddy to experiment with—it was more than I could bear to know. It felt as if it was easier not to know, until now. I'm 54 years old, and the pain feels as fresh, as new as if it had happened yesterday, rather than 50 years ago. I have hopes that writing this will help ease the pain and bring some peace. I wonder if it will.

At this writing, my daughter, who is now an adult with two daughters of her own, is helping me to edit my work. She tells me that I need to know more about his treatments and how he died—that I need more detail on the electric shock treatments.

She tells me it is my responsibility as a writer. She says it feels like I left out parts that were too painful. As tears slide down my cheeks unchecked, I realize she must be right, otherwise why does it hurt me so to talk about it, to think about it? I know that I must go deeper into the wound and deeper into understanding what they did to Daddy while he was in the hospital, and I know that this is going to bring me much pain. My hope is that someone will gain from my pain; otherwise maybe those who say to just leave sleeping dogs lie are right and all this delving into me has been for no reason.

So, as my daughter advised I did some research and what I found appalls me. Not only was this the treatment in the 50s, but ECT is still practiced today—and still without prior consent in some states. Insulin Coma Therapy (ICT) Therapy was discontinued in this country in the early 1960s. "After years of decline, shock therapy is making a dramatic and sometimes deadly comeback, practiced now mostly on depressed elderly women who are largely ignorant of shock's true dangers and misled about shock's real risks" (Research-Able Inc., 1998). While I do not want to turn this book into a thesis for or against the practice of Electroconvulsive (ECT) Therapy, I believe that we need to become aware of what is happening and what has happened. (See Appendix for more information on this treatment.)

In my research, I learned that my Daddy would have been given these shock treatments with no prior consent, with no anesthetic, no pain medication, and no muscle relaxant, so he would have felt, and felt violently, every shock they gave to his brain. His body would have convulsed, writhing in horrible pain as he suffered the total invasion of his mind and body privacy. What a horrific way to die! They used our Daddy as an experiment, and it killed him. Then, without any explanation or offer of help, they left Mama with nine kids to support. Our Daddy was a living human being who had a nervous breakdown from too much stress, and then medical experimentation killed him.

As I said, my memories of my Daddy are of him in his coffin, not hugging me or holding me or laughing and playing with me. He never got the chance to do any of that when I would have been old enough to remember. I can see him so clearly that all I have to do is close my eyes and he is there.

Dark olive complexion big strong high cheekbones curly dark hair not old enough when he died for there to be any gray in his hair.

What a shame who's to blame?

Full lips large squat nose a handsome fellow was he.

Wide forehead looked intelligent not old enough when he died for there to be any gray in his hair what a shame who's to blame?

Because I have seen pictures of him in his coffin, I couldn't say for sure that I remember the actual coffin or the picture—it is a blur to me—I just know either from the photograph or in my mind's eye that I see him. Oh how I see him.

In the South at that time, when someone died, their body was brought home to "lie in wait" for three days before they were buried. All the family went to the house with lots of food and stayed up all night with the immediate family. So as was the custom, Daddy's body rested in his coffin in our living room.

Several of us kids, my twin sister Berline, my sister Ruth, who was two years older, and my younger brother James, who was three years younger than I, went out to the barn for something. While we were out there Ruth lost her shoe, so we set out to find it. Thinking that maybe it had fallen in the cracks in the floor and was under the barn, we lit a match to try to see it. There was tobacco in the barn as it was the time of year to sort, tie and then haul the sorted dry tobacco to the market to be sold. While I cannot quite remember whose hand held the match, I remember that someone accidentally hit that person's hand and the lit match dropped onto the dry tobacco. It only took a moment for the fire to start. Despite our fear, we were certain that we could just get some buckets of water and extinguish the blaze, but of course we could not.

My older brothers and sisters were in the house watching television, which was so new to us that once in front of it, you became somewhat mesmerized by it. By the time they heard us yelling and saw the flames it was too late. The barn went up in a roar of fire and flames that could be seen for miles. There was a lot of running around, as kids will do, yelling at each other, one blaming the other and all of us scared. Us younger ones because of what we had done, and the older ones because they knew they should have been watching us rather than television, so they would also get some blame. We were all screaming and running around like chickens with their heads cut off, carrying buckets as fast as our little legs could move, trying to put out the fire until finally, it was no use.

We each, in our own private hell, waited for Mama to come home from town, where she'd most likely gone to make Daddy's funeral arrangements. The barn burned down with my Daddy lying in his coffin in the living room. So much work, so much he had died for and now it was all gone up in smoke.

My twin sister Berline and I were so scared of getting in trouble that we climbed up into the coffin with Daddy, thinking if we looked pitiful enough, the grown-ups would feel sorry for us instead of mad. That's where his sisters, our aunts, found us. We cried and cried, I think more because we were afraid of getting into trouble, not because Daddy was "asleep" in the coffin. I wonder if this was the beginning of the feeling of standing outside myself and watching, always watching, watching the pain "that little girl" was feeling but not feeling it, oh no, not feeling it. I became exceptionally good at pushing the pain away and hiding it inside, pretending it did not exist.

Isn't it strange that at four years old I didn't understand my Daddy was gone, but I understood that if we could get sympathy from my aunts, Mama would not get too angry with us? That we could and did manipulate the situation so that my aunts told our Mama what we had done, how upset we were, and how much we had cried. I can hear them; I can see Mama sitting in the corner listening to them, looking at us. Poor Mama, maybe she would have felt better if she could have taken some anger out on us, who knows. How is it, I can remember being manipulative at such a young age, but cannot remember my Daddy holding me?

Through all the years that followed, Mama would sing us a song that seemed to capture exactly how we felt about losing Daddy. "How Far is Heaven". If I just close my eyes, I can hear her singing it to us still and us kids singing along with her.

A little girl was waiting for her Daddy one day
It was time to meet him, and she heard her mommy say
Come to mommy, darling, please do not cry
Daddy's gone to Heaven away up in the sky.

How far is Heaven, when can I go
To see my Daddy, he's there I know
How far is Heaven, let's go tonight
I want my Daddy to hold me tight.

He was gone so suddenly, I could not say goodbye
I know that he's in Heaven; we'll meet him by and by.
The little girl she trembled, her tears she could not hide
She looked up towards Heaven, and then she replied,

How far is Heaven, when can I go
To see my Daddy, he's there I know
How far is Heaven, let's go tonight
I want my Daddy to hold me tight,
I want my Daddy to hold me tight.

CHAPTER 2
THE WOLVES COME OUT

I have found that it is never just about losing a loved one in death; it is also about the changes in your life that are brought about because that person is no longer there. And boy, did our lives change! Do you remember Merle Haggard's song "Mama Tried"? That pretty much says it all: Mama tried to keep the farm, keep us whole, and keep us fed and clothed and safe from all the harm that seemed to come our way. When I say "wolves," I mean the grown men who took advantage of Mama, and of us children—girls and boys alike—sometimes through violence, sometimes through force, but always through the loss of safety no child should ever experience. But she was a young woman with eight kids and one on the way when Daddy died, and no matter how hard she tried, she could not keep us safe. She could not give us all that we needed to be whole, unscathed by the life we would lead and the people who would laugh at us and take advantage of us just because they could.

Now that I'm older and have gone through my own hardships in life, I have some small knowledge of what life must have been like for her, and it's hard for me to imagine how she remained sane and able to take even minimal care of all of us.

It seemed there was always a lot of fighting and arguing. The younger kids had their battles, and the older group fought their own battles. My older brothers were 14 and 13 at the time of Daddy's death. These brothers took seriously their responsibilities of being the men left in the house, and therefore, with their differing opinions, they fought a lot: about the farm, how to run it, how to take care of Mama and us kids. How awful all that must have been for Mama. All of us fighting, her trying to take care of us, and trying to run the farm, and of course, finally, trying to figure out how to feed us.

She was a very pretty woman—red hair, blue eyes—and as a single woman with no man to protect her, she became fair game for all my uncles and any other man that was within the area. They wanted to "take care of her," or rather, take care of her sexual needs because in their stupidity, they assumed she would want that! Sometimes I wish I could go back and hurt them as much as they had hurt my Mama. It must have been awful to be grieving Daddy, desperate for money, nine kids to care for in every way with no help, and them after her to bed her, all for her own good of course. Anyway, she sold the farm, and of course none of the good uncles helped her get a good price, so she didn't. We moved into town and so life began in all its glory. But I'm getting ahead of myself—I better back up some to after Daddy died and before we moved into town.

Thereafter followed the cruelties that life had to offer in Daddy's absence—not just him, but what he represented: safety. There were so many cruelties that maybe not all of them bear mentioning. Maybe I cannot bear to remember them all again.

Sometime after Daddy died and before we moved into town, when I was between ages 4 and 6 years (approximately 1957-1959), I was introduced to experiences no child should know. I cannot tell you exactly what they were for sure, but I could probably remember in some detail if I let myself. Sometimes maybe some things are just better left hidden inside. I learned to do that a lot in my life, just hide the hurt inside if it was too hard to face the light of day. All I remember is being in the woods with my sisters, although which ones I do not recall, and some of my boy cousins. I remember we girls were made to lie on the ground in the sand with the trees all around us, and to remove our underclothes. The details fade into darkness there, and for now we will leave it that way.

I do know that these episodes happened more than once. I have no idea how many times, and I guess that's ok with me. I just know that I felt dirty, unclean, like I was a bad little girl. I was a little girl with no control in her life and no control over what was happening to her. Those feelings would stay with me the rest of my life and come back to lead me into decisions many times to find ways to put myself into a safe place so that I wouldn't be that bad little girl.

During that time, most of us kids went to Sunday school—I can't remember if Mama did or not; someone either picked us up or we went by bus. I loved church and during this time that my relationship with God began. A relationship that has been a part of me through out my life. I wish I could tell you that having that relationship made everything in my life good and ok, but it didn't. It did, however, give me the knowledge that someone was always there, even in the darkest times, and gave me a hunger to be a "good girl." Who knows who or what I might have become without this relationship and hunger for God in me? I also wish I could tell you that all the people in the church were the vision of God Himself, but that also is not true. People are people wherever you find them, and some will be nice and some not so nice. There were kids in church who laughed at us because we had no daddy and we were poor, just like there were kids at school who did the same. Because my expectations were higher for the people in church, those cuts were somehow crueler and deeper.

I started first grade while we still lived in the country on our farm. My memories are of feeling ashamed and poor and never good enough. We seemed to be outcasts, different because we didn't have a daddy. I wanted a daddy so bad, a daddy to love me and take care of me, like all the other kids had. I can't recount the times I cried wanting a daddy, wanting to be like them, not wanting to be poor, and for sure not wanting hand-outs. Most of all I just wanted to fit in—be like the other kids.

Sometimes I stepped outside myself and watched this little girl —watched myself. She tried so hard to be good and so desperately wanted to be loved. I watched her go to great lengths to be accepted, and to do most anything so the kids wouldn't tease her. I felt her fears and lack of understanding when she felt so much shame and didn't know why. She couldn't understand why her daddy's dying brought so much shame, like suddenly without a daddy, she was damaged goods. She thought if she could just be good enough, she would be lovable and not that poor girl who had no daddy and no money for lunches. Well, she tried, but it didn't work. They still teased her, and now they just called her Miss-Goody-Two-Shoes, and they still did not love her. Sometimes I just stayed outside for a while.

We were all so full of pain, my sisters, brothers and I, and so young, we had no idea how to help ourselves and certainly not each other. And poor Mama, she had a farm to run, men to try and keep away; and nine kids to feed; there was no time for anything else.

We moved into town, we got welfare; Mama worked, but of course she could never tell the welfare people she was working; then they would not give us any money, and even though it wasn't enough, we needed everything we could get.

I wonder: did we all start to die then? Was that the beginning, or did we all start to die when Daddy died and was no longer there to protect us?

I spoke to my sister Ruth today. Ruth is in a wheelchair and has been for several years now. She has rheumatoid arthritis and is totally dependent on her husband for food, to go to the bathroom, to help her get dressed, for all her normal everyday needs. Most of her time is spent in unbearable pain, and what is not is spent doped up on drugs to kill the pain. She and her husband have become homebound, isolated and lonely. They both have great faith in God, which is the only thing that seems to keep them going, but even so, their lives have become almost unbearable. She is one of two sisters that I have left here on earth, and I'm not sure how much longer she will be here. She is just two years older than I.

As we talk, I'm afraid I don't have much time to ask her questions about her past, and about how our Daddy's death affected her.

"Ruth?" I asked, "What was your life like for you as a girl? I want to know what your experiences were like and if you felt this feeling of being apart, of separating out and observing your life."

Ruth responded, "It is really better to leave the past in the past. I suppose we all feel a little like we are just watchers sometimes."

Feeling a little frustrated that she would try to get me to just leave things alone because that is the decision she had made in her life, I persisted with a few questions. I also knew she was very sick and I needed to be careful not to push too much. I proceeded gently to ask her what her feelings had been with the other kids at school after Daddy died.

"There was a girl who laughed at me because I did not have a daddy," she said. I could hear the pain that was still in her voice.

"I hated her so much that for many years all I could think of was going back and hurting her."

Ruth let out a little laugh at herself and continued.

"Funny I do not even remember who she was but I hated her for years. I finally had to work at forgiving her so that it didn't eat at me; and Daddy dying, well not having a daddy meant the wolves came around, you know, everything else hinged on it, Daddy dying." She spoke quietly.

I sat for a few minutes, filled with pain and almost shock, it seems. I'm not sure what I thought she'd say. I knew that, for all these years, those had been my words: wolves coming around, and now to hear her speaking to them told me that she had endured the same pain—who knew what the "wolves" had done to her. I wanted to ask, but I knew it would be very painful for her and for me, more painful than either of us could bear today, so I let it go.

"But" she continued in a tired voice, "do not go back, you have already felt the pain, you do not need to feel it again."

As my throat got tight and my chest hurt with keeping the tears away, I thought, maybe she is right! But while she was talking, the oddest thought came to my mind, like one of those intuitive pops I sometimes get, she is still feeling the pain, every day in her body, her body cannot let go of the pain. Who knows if this is the truth, but to me it was a very real and true thing.

Death can be a slow process sometimes, and sometimes your body is living but you are dead already. I knew that, for me, as painful as this process is, I must continue this journey into my past, our past, our pain.

I let it go for the day and waited for another time to ask her a few more questions. When an opportunity arose, I ventured into the questions again.

"Ruth," I asked, "what was I like as a child?" and "Did you ever stand outside and look in?"

Ruth took her responsibilities as the older sister in earnest and I could hear that in the measured way she replied, "I think it is normal to stand outside and look in, I'm sure everyone does that sometimes."

I was somehow not convinced though; I knew she wouldn't want me to feel abnormal, but I was also left to wonder if she had indeed felt this way. She didn't elaborate and I didn't push anymore. Years ago, when I was going through divorce, I remember talking to my counselor about being normal, wanting normal for my kids, and I remember him saying there is no normal. I believe that to be true.

I have never asked anyone else about this being on the outside looking in, this observer that is a part of me. Maybe in this journey I will ask, maybe there is a name for it, a reason for it. Maybe everyone does do it or maybe it is my escape hatch; no matter now, it has been a part of me as long as I can remember.

I had gotten lost in thought and brought myself back as Ruth continued.

"I do remember the time you seemed to go off on the deep end." Knowing that was our Southern term for a nervous breakdown, I listened to what she remembered.

"For a period of some time, I think it was a couple of years, you would cry a lot, scream and be afraid of anything that moved. Even a broom, we couldn't even sweep when you were around. You were afraid of your own shadow, and after a while the rest of the kids were all mad at you. You were getting all the attention, and we were getting none."

As she talked, the memories came flooding back to me. I remember my older brother Gaston asking me if I was faking it. We were lying on a bed together and he had his arms around me, it felt so good for him to be nice to me and to feel loved. I believe by this time that my sister was right, that I was out of the hole I had been in enough to know that I could come out if I wanted to, but I was not sure I wanted to.

While I was in this deep dark hole I do remember getting more attention, and in a family of nine, that felt pretty good. I remember Mama taking me to what I know now was a university hospital where we saw a team of doctors. I was put in a chair in the front of a room with a bunch of doctors asking me all kinds of questions. I have no idea what they asked, or, of course, what I answered. But I do know that for a while I was special; Mama was there and giving me the best thing she could have—her time.

Why can't I ever remember Mama hugging me as a child? Did she hug me, and I just forgot? Mamas need to hug their babies. Isn't that a song? Well so they do! But then I'm not sure my Mama had much time to hug, what with nine kids to feed and clothe and her all by herself to do it.

Now that I'm an adult I have to wonder: Why would any group of doctors who were trying to help a 6-year-old girl put her in a room full of doctors like a specimen to be studied? This was just one more episode to prove that I was a little girl who did not matter. It seems that somewhere in me I've always known that was such a stupid thing to do. We lived on welfare so of course we didn't matter, did we, we were just part of the system, so they didn't need to help me. After all, they could study me if they wanted to since we were not paying. Sound a little bitter, don't I? Well, maybe a little.

The helping system can be so cruel and not even realize it. Anyway, over time, I got better. Now I know it was because my Mama gave me some special attention and the love that I needed so that enough of the pain would go away for me to come out and play again in the real world.

As an adult now with many experiences behind me, I know that I was just a very sensitive child who needed love and attention, and most of all needed to be liked and accepted. At that time, it was just a whole big world of not fitting in. Wow, no wonder we have boys who spin out of control in teenage years. When you are very sensitive and feel like you are an outcast for any reason, it puts a hole in you that can cause all kinds of emotions, pain, and unhealthy ways of coping.

My mind had strayed, so I had been silent for a while. Ruth's next words brought me crashing back.

"I think your breakdown had something to do with our uncle that used to come and stay at our house."

A mixture of feelings convulsed my whole body. I'm sure she didn't know the turmoil she had just unleashed in me: anger, hurt, and this feeling of being ripped apart inside. Hot seething anger at my uncles for what they had done to me and now to know it was these incidents with them that had caused me to go over the edge. It was all I could do to keep from screaming out. I had been able to remember some of what happened during the time of my "mental breakdown" but what I had not remembered was that it was due to my uncles and what they did to me, and what I learned in later years they had also done to my other sisters. These two uncles would come to our house drunk, needing somewhere to sleep it off. But their version of "getting warm" in our beds consisted of touching us in ways that made us feel dirty and ashamed.

Sometimes when the "wolves" came over to get warm, I'd slip out of bed and run into another room. That left my twin sister Berline, my brother James, and my little sister Roma, in bed with the wolves. While my adult mind knows that I didn't know what else to do, didn't mean for them to be hurt, and didn't know how to save myself or them, my child brain carries a lot of guilt for leaving them with the "wolf." I wonder how many times I wished those wolves dead. When I heard of their deaths, my only feeling was one of relief and satisfaction.

As Ruth and I continued our conversation that day she spoke of how Berline and I had gotten married so young and 'escaped' from home.

"After all," she said, "the wolves could come over at any time."

I shudder to think of what she and my other two older sisters, Bertha and Carol, had to endure in their lives, when "after all, the wolves could come over at any time." Which of course meant that they had, and that they'd wreaked havoc in my sisters' lives as well. Evil seems to not care on whom he calls.

Carol and Bertha are both gone now, and I'm not sure if I'd ask them if I could. I'm not sure that I, or they, could bear the pain of remembering and then talking about it. I can hardly bear the pain of thinking of it now.

We had moved into the small town of Clinton and lived in a nice big white house where I thought we would have a "normal" life. I was attending a neighborhood church and there developed a friendship with a little neighbor girl. I wanted so desperately to fit in, to be ok, to have "normal" friends. This little girl had a Mama and a Daddy and to me she had everything in life that was important. I was sure she was safe from the wolves and most of all she had a Mama and a Daddy. This friendship was like life itself to me. But I knew things that she did not, and as kids will do, I shared some of those things with her. I told her that I knew how babies came; I knew what men did to women to get babies. So, innocent in my mind, but in her mother's eyes I was no longer someone who was 'fit' to play with her little girl.

Even though I tried to tell her mother how sorry I was, how I really was a good little girl, I really did not mean to say those things, it was too late, and I was not allowed to play with my friend again. I was devastated. I couldn't understand why I was such a bad, dirty little girl. No matter what I did, the shame and dirt always stayed with me. Her mother confirmed that I was nobody, a nothing, a bad girl, a poor girl, a girl who good girls should not have anything to do with. This guilt I carried as a child, for what my uncles kept doing to me every chance they got, and for leaving my sisters and brothers with them, was all too much. I left my body for a while. No one could hurt me if I was not there.

As I write, I wonder why God allowed my Daddy to die. Why did He allow the death that left us to the wolves, and why did He allow each and every painful death after that? I'm who I am because of where I have come from, and while today I can say, I like who I am well enough, it could have been easier, and one does have to sometimes wonder why. Why not make it easier, why allow so many painful episodes in our lives? I'm not feeling sorry for myself as I realize that terrible things happen to many people. But knowing that does not make my pain any less real. And if I do not tell the story, you will not know and maybe there is some reason for you to know.

As I sit this morning having my coffee, I hear the taunts, "Your daddy's crazy, your daddy's crazy, your daddy's crazy," and I know that these are the taunts I heard from other kids at school. While I cannot remember any one person, I can hear the taunts and see the stares of the teachers and other adults. They look at us as if they expect us to "go crazy" at any minute. We are tainted goods, we have bad blood, and we forever live with the stigma of having a father who "went crazy." Just today I realized why there was always such shame in our lives.

Yesterday was a tough day for me as I wrote about Mama. I cried a good part of the day. Then as I went to bed last night, worn out from all the emotion, the thoughts came, nipping at my mind, tugging at the memories. Like a game of hide and seek. You can't catch me, you can't catch me, find me if you can. I'm here now behind this tree, now I'm under the bed; catch me if you can.

I had hidden a part of the truth from myself all these years. It wasn't only about losing Daddy, being laughed at for not having a daddy—that was only part of the pain. The worst part of the jeers had been "Your daddy went crazy," and the worst part of the fears was that, if he went crazy, then maybe I will as well. There was the laughter of the other kids at school, but worse were the stares of the teachers and the little snippets of information I heard them whispering when they saw me. Teachers were like God, if they thought we were tainted then we must be. I must be. I must be going to lose my mind like Daddy—the teachers thought so. It must be true.

That was what some of the pain and the shame was about. We were pointed at, talked about, laughed at—the stigma hung over us that our Daddy went crazy. No wonder I tried to be such a good little girl. I tried to control everyone and everything around me. I tried to run and hide from the shame and the pain. So tragic, that it has taken me 54 years to remember this seemingly small piece of information that has had such a huge influence on my life. I had hidden it from myself all these years. I wonder how many decisions I have made through the years based on the fear of losing my mind, of going crazy like Daddy, of being tainted goods.

So, the inability to accept myself all these years, to trust who I am and who I was, to know that I was smart, that I had something to offer has all been based in part on the shame and the fear that our Daddy went crazy and if he did, then I might as well. That I was tarnished goods, that something was wrong with us as a family.

When I look at us now, I realize how intelligent we are, and were: my brothers who started and ran very successful businesses, our minds that don't stop, that are always thinking and coming up with ideas. We were all like this and in some households, we would have been considered to have brilliant minds, and given lots of encouragement to live life, to succeed, to try things, and to create. Instead, I grew up thinking I was not creative and that something was wrong with me because I have a mind that won't shut down. A mind that can come up with more ideas in a day than most can come up with in a lifetime.

I saw Maria Shriver on Oprah a few weeks ago and she talked about how her dad had always encouraged her and had told her she could be anything she wanted to be. I could not help but feel jealous of her for having had a father and especially one who had encouraged her all through her life. I wonder what or who we could have been with that kind of encouragement.

So my writing has helped me in some way. There is somehow a freedom in the knowledge of understanding how my Daddy died even though I still do not want to allow myself to think about it too much. The truth is, Daddy didn't just die—he was a patient in an experimental medical program that went wrong. In those days, people with mental illness were often treated like lab rats, subjected to treatments that were more about advancing medical knowledge than helping the patient. Whatever they did to him in that institution killed him at age 33. The shame we felt wasn't just about having a "crazy" father—it was about being the children of a man who died because doctors treated him like he didn't matter.

Now, finally knowing why we would have felt so much shame, along with our pain at Daddy's death, brings me some measure of peace. I had hidden away inside the jeers and the stares of the kids and other adults who seemed to know no better than to treat us as damaged goods because our Daddy had died in a mental institution. Those pieces that had been too painful for me to admit to myself, I had just hidden away inside. Now out in the open, they lose some of their sting and I understand why, years later, when I was going to therapy to help me through my marriage to an alcoholic husband, I cried my eyes out for two days without stopping after watching a video of a little girl hiding behind a door to get away from her pain.

Our Daddy had died in a mental institution, died due to a mistake of medical experimentation, but the stigma was there nonetheless, and the pain was too much to bear for this little girl. But that little girl survived. She found ways to protect herself, even when no one else could.

CHAPTER 3

MAMA'S LIFE WITHOUT DADDY

My Mama was a strong woman— a fiery redhead. One story illustrates her temper when aroused. The "cat" story was told many times around Mama's kitchen table—our family gathering place. Watching Mama's face each time we brought up "the cat story" was an event. She would sit there with a look that said she did not understand why we all found this so funny; to her it made perfect sense. Wringing that cat's neck!

I'm not totally clear on how many of us had been born by then but suffice it to say Mama had several kids running around to feed, wash clothes for, and take care of. She also worked in the tobacco and cotton fields with Daddy, then cooked for all of us and cleaned the house.

On this day, she had just finished washing clothes, which was no easy task at the time—we had one of the old wringer washing machines, so doing the laundry meant more than just plopping the clothes in the machine and letting the machine do the rest.

The old wringer washers would wash the clothes, but then you had to run them by hand through two rollers at the top of the machine to squeeze the water out, then into a tub of water to rinse them, and then back through the rollers again. Afterwards, the clothes had to be hung outside on the clothesline to dry. For a family the size of ours, washing clothes was a good half-day job. Mama had finished her big wash, hung them out to dry, and when dry, brought them in and put them on the bed to be folded later.

Hurrying to get dinner done before Daddy came in from the fields, she left them there for a short while. So there those clothes lay, all clean and fresh, when one of the barn cats decided to come in for a nap—and then pooped all over the fresh clean clothes on the bed. When Mama found them, they were a mess of course and had to be redone. Mama saw red and began yelling and screaming at the cat; I'm sure the poor thing was scared almost to death with this shrieking redheaded woman chasing after him. He darted under the house to escape, but that didn't deter my Mama. She crawled right under that little house, wrapped her fingers around the cat's scrawny neck, and began choking him. Luckily for him he got away and I'm pretty sure he never showed his face again at our farm. Even writing this story makes me laugh, thinking of Mama chasing that cat under the house.

Our Mama was a gentle, fun-loving woman in many ways, but we knew better than to cross her when she told us to do something. When Mama set her mind to something, she usually found a way to do it. I have no doubt that if she'd been given the opportunity of an education, she could have gone far. As it was, life dealt her a hand, and she played it to the best of her ability.

In my mind's eye, I can picture Mama standing in the sunshine with one or two of the old wooden clothespins in her mouth, her apron billowing in the breeze, pinning the corners of a brightly colored shirt to the clothesline. I miss the old clotheslines with their freshly washed bounty hanging in the sun, the warm southern breeze softly wafting through, making the sheets billow first up, and then down, waving gently like a ghost coming to say hello.

Mama's mama, Mary Victoria, died when Mama was born. Her Dad already had several kids and could not care for Mama, so he sent her to live with Mary Victoria's two spinster sisters. Mama never really knew her father. When he remarried, he went back to get Mama, but by that time, her aunts wouldn't let her go, so she lived with them, with no sisters and brothers. I have often wondered what that was like for Mama, and if she felt abandoned by her daddy.

At age sixteen she and my Daddy were married (around 1938); Daddy would have been eighteen. When he died at age 33, there were already eight of us kids and one more on the way, so their lives must have been very busy, to say the least. Mama would only have been 32 years old with 8 kids to support in every way when Daddy died. When I look back it always seemed that Mama was old and even the first writing of this book, I was still looking back with my young eyes thinking and remembering as the child. Now in the updating of this book I know that Mama was quite young when Daddy died and left her with all the responsibilities. My goodness that would have broken most people. What a strong woman she was.

The story goes that when my twin sister and I were born, Mama was at home, and her delivery had been long and difficult. Not knowing she was having twins and exhausted from several hours in labor, by the time we arrived she just didn't care what our names would be, so she let the midwife name us. We were named Earline and Berline, and if our names had any significance, it must have been from the midwife. Berline was ten minutes older than I. Now Mama had two babies and five other kids to take care of along with working in the fields. No wonder she was so strong; she had no choice if she wanted to survive.

Twins

Berline and Earline twins we are named. Coming at the same time as two who are called. Called for what We knew not.

We are what we are we were what we were; not one but two, not two but one.

Together we are bound together we have found our life to be hard, our life to be sad.

But always we were glad that together we had not one but two, not two but one.

She looked like Daddy I looked like Mama; she was quiet and I was the talker she was the tough one I was the worrying one, she was the dark one, I was the light one she was the wild one, and I the shy one.

She chased my brother up a tree Butcher knife in hand; she was
a fighter and so was he.

She married and had boys I married and had girls; she stayed in
the South I moved to the West.

I didn't know it and neither did she, but she would be the sick
one and I the guilty one as death took its toll on her and me.

For a while we were together, called as Twins not one but two,
not two but one, Berline and Earline.

Three years later my brother James was born, and little more
than a year later, Daddy died, and Mama was three months
pregnant with my sister Roma. I can't imagine how she must
have felt: pregnant, with seven other kids running around, a
farm to run, and Daddy dead. It was springtime then, so the
fields would need to be plowed, and the new tobacco planted.
The plow horses needed caring for, the garden to plant our food
would have needed plowing, and Mama still had us seven kids
before Roma was born, to cook for, clean for, and in general do
all that kids would need to have done when they are too little to
take care of themselves. Mama was 32, a young woman to be
left alone with eight kids and one on the way.

My memories of Daddy's family are vague and filled with dread,
fear, and revulsion. There seemed to be big black secrets that
hung over my grandparents' house. I have no recollection what-
soever of my grandparents ever hugging me or feeling any love
or safety in their house.

Other feelings rise to the surface as I write, some that are hard to
identify: stress, fear, dislike, but not love. Then there were the

whispers and fears of being called into Grandpa's room with
him. The ROOM, the big black scary room. Instinctively we
knew that it was a place we did not want to go. We didn't even
want to visit them at all.

All that comes back is a bad taste in my mouth and a dread in
my heart. I never sensed any love there, only feelings that were
dark, secrets that we dared not talk about. It still gives me a knot
in the pit of my stomach to think of that time and that place.
The only way I remember my grandmother was with her
standing in front of the old cast iron potbelly wood stove with
her skirt hiked up in back to get warm. She and my grandfather
always seemed to be judging my Mama and trying to tell her
what to do.

Some of my Daddy's family seemed to be awful people or that is
what we felt. Mama hated them; I know that even though I
cannot remember her telling me so. I felt it, sensed it, and knew
it to be true. Knew there was something vile in the family that
she wanted to get away from and stay away from. Once we
moved into town, I never remember visiting my grandparents
again. We did visit some of the family but never them. Sometime after Daddy died she made the decision to sell the farm
and move away; a decision I'm sure they wouldn't have agreed
with. My older brothers were angry with her about selling the
farm, but they were young and would not have understood how
hard it would be to keep the farm profitable and get the work
done without Daddy's help.

I felt such hatred for them, even as I write this, that it comes into
the pit of my stomach and threatens to pour out. I understand

some of it but not all. There was something dark and hidden along with the constant judging of Mama and the men always wanting to "look out after Mama"

As I write this story and allow myself to think about my life growing up in the South, I understand increasingly why I always wanted to be away from that place, that time, and to run, always run from the past, always thinking I was a nothing, a nobody, that I was dirty.

I believe that my Daddy was a kind and loving man. I know that he loved us, somehow, I know that, and I know that Mama loved him, so whoever he was he had to be someone of value or Mama would not have loved him. He was sensitive, caring—maybe caring too much to handle all the stress and strain.

Throughout my life I have come to know that I'm very sensitive; I see and know things around me that sometimes other people do not see. I sense feelings underneath the surface, and even when I don't always understand them, I know when something is wrong, when something is amiss. There have been enough instances in my life of "knowing things" for me to trust this in myself today. Many times, I have seen things before they happen. While my memory may fail me, I'm sure of the darkness, the secrets, and the cruelty that we all felt during this time.

Some fragments of stories, some bits pull at my mind and heart: of the brother who beat his wife and kids and whose kids became mean and nasty, just like their dad. Of the married men that you always had to be wary of, and who you knew inside yourself that you should never be alone with. Somehow just being in the same room with them made you feel dirty, and we knew they were constantly after my Mama.

Mama broke some of that chain of darkness for us when she sold the farm and moved us into town. Some, not all! She knew and was smart enough to keep them away from her and us. My Mama was a great woman, a woman of pride, conviction, and perseverance. It's too bad I didn't know it then, to tell her how much I appreciated what she was able to do for us, instead of doing as children will do, and making her feel bad for what we did not have. I hope she knows now how much I appreciate all her sacrifices for us.

But Mama found ways to make even the hardest times bearable. To support ourselves after we moved into town, we worked in the tobacco fields in the summer. During the winter, we worked on the dried tobacco in the two rooms in our rented house where we stored it. The green tobacco had to be "cropped" off the stalk in the field and then tied to a stick that was then put into a barn for curing time. After curing, it would be taken off the stick and graded into stacks according to its quality. In the summer, as Mama drove us down to the farms, she sang songs to us and we'd all sing along on the way down. I remember one song in particular: Sugar in the Morning.

Sugar in the morning

Sugar in the evening

Sugar at suppertime.

Be my little sugar

And love me all the time.

Well sugar time

Is anytime that you are near

Or just appear.

Be my little sugar

And love me all the time.

Mama was always singing, even with her hard life she was always singing. Those were hard times, but good times, and I have a lot of happy memories of being in the car with Mama and her singing, of working hard in the tobacco fields and feeling good, even though bone weary tired at the end of the day. Some farms where we worked provided wonderful "dinners," which was our midday meal, and at some farms we brought our own meal. Even better were the times we got to stop at the store on the way down and buy nabs and drinks, as we called them, along with oatmeal cakes and the like for lunch. Those were some of the best tasting treats I can remember eating. I still love oatmeal cakes and nabs, which are crackers and cheese or crackers and peanut butter.

I hadn't thought about it much until now, but Mama passed her love of singing on to me. When my girls were growing up and we drove anywhere in the car, we always sang songs. It was always so much fun to ride and sing together, both with Mama and with my own daughters. My granddaughters are all good singers and my daughters are as well.

As we harvested in the summer, the green tobacco stained our hands until they were dark with tobacco. There were always watermelons in the fields, and I remember many times going to the watermelon fields and dashing one to the ground so that it would break open, then we'd dig out the heart from its center and eat it with our hands, all stained and dirty from the tobacco. The first bite or so would be bitter and black and sticky from our hands, but after that, the juice washed some of the bitter tobacco off, and the melon tasted so sweet and fresh. Sweeter and better than any candy one could possibly buy. The sun was hot and the watermelon warm and sweet—those are pleasant memories.

There was always a barn full of us working; corporations today could learn a lot about building a team by the way we worked together in those fields. We had croppers who went out into the fields and cropped the leaves off the stalks and put them in horse- or tractor-drawn wagons. When the wagons were full, they'd drag them up to the barn where the rest of us worked at getting the green tobacco leaves onto sticks to be put into the warmed barns for curing. The 'handers' would bunch three or four of the tobacco leaves together and hand them to the 'tiers,' who then tied the leaves onto the stick, which was about 5 or 6 feet long and stood up on wooden cross bow type things to hold them up. The tiers had to be very fast because we had four or five handers per tier, and the tier had to tie the bunches of tobacco to the stick until the stick was full. Once full, the sticks were piled on top of each other until it was time to put them all in the barn, where they were left until they were dry, or cured. The tiers and the croppers seemed to have the most stature and we handers always wanted to work up to being the tier or crop-per. We always felt honored when we were good enough to move up in rank. What fun we had as we worked and talked and gossiped and worked!

In the winter months, we had to take the dried tobacco sticks out of the storage rooms in our house at night and lay them on the grass around our house. Then we'd get up before dawn, before the dew fell on the tobacco, and pick all the sticks up again and bring them into the house to be graded. I hated getting up early in the morning to go pick up those sticks. Mama always had to yell at us. What a chore that must have been—getting us up and out the door! We were all very crabby with each other as I remember, fighting about who had to do what.

It always seemed like we had a big enough house. But with eight kids at home with Mama and never living in a house probably much larger than 1100 square feet, I'm sure what seemed big enough was small. We were always four or five to a bed, and at night we told each other scary stories. I never remember thinking I wanted my own bed, though, let alone my own room. It just wasn't even a possibility, so it didn't enter my mind. This was the way Mama supported us for years, or the way we supported ourselves. I also don't remember ever thinking that the money we made was mine. We all worked, and Mama got the earnings and supported us with it.

She was always "figuring," as she called it—paying bills and wondering where the next meal was coming from. One of the ways I remember her most was at the kitchen table with a pen and paper doing her figuring. My sister Roma spent some time living with me this past year and she said, "Girl, you remind me of Mama, always figuring." I hadn't seen the comparison but I'm sure it's true; I'm always figuring too. If not bills, then something else, whatever my mind is working on that day.

After a while we didn't do tobacco anymore although I'm not sure why, but we stopped. Then Mama went to work in nursing homes. She hated the places but loved the people in them. She always told us to never put her in one of those homes, and the fear of them is something she passed on to us.

While she was at work, Mama left some of the older sisters in charge of us younger ones, and those are the only times I remember anyone ever really disciplining me. If that is what you could call it. When any of us were fighting or bickering, my older sister would get a switch and make us hit each other or hug each other around the neck. Boy, we hated both of those things. We might fight with each other all the time, but to be forced to hit each other was something none of us could bear. So of course, at these times we'd run away, which only made her mad, and then she'd call Mama and sometimes Mama would have to come home. That was the worst of it—if she had to come home, then she would cry. Making Mama cry made us feel lower than dirt.

But kids being kids, we continued to fight. I still carry a scar down my breast from fighting on the kitchen floor with my brother. I would fight to a certain point, but many times my brother and sister would go well past that point. My twin sister ran my brother up trees with butcher knives many times, and I have no doubt that if she'd been able to catch him, she would have hurt him.

The other punishment my older sister doled out was making us stand, facing the sibling we'd been fighting with, and hugging them around the neck. We would try to just barely touch the other person because of course at the time, we thought we just hated them. But stand we would, with our arms around each other. It's funny now to think of it.

All the years we were growing up, my sisters and I used the term 'beat you to death.' "I'm going to beat you to death." I used that slang for years without even thinking about what it meant. We must have looked so funny to outsiders—or so pathetic. After moving out to the west coast and having kids one of my friends said something to me about using that term and I thought it so funny that anyone would think it was a bad thing to say but then realized that indeed it certainly was not the best slang, so I stopped using it.

Mama got welfare while she worked in the rest homes, always struggling to make enough to feed and clothe us, always on guard not to let the authorities know she was working; otherwise, they would have taken away what help they gave. What they gave was not enough, and what Mama was able to make working was not enough, so one without the other was less than we could survive on. The two together was barely survival mode. Lord, she must have been tired, working full time and taking care of us. How her pride must have been hurt, bowing down to the authorities to get handouts of commodity food, some of which you wondered if it was even fit to eat, and a little money to help us survive. We got some help with medical, although not much. I could just scream with the pain of what she had to endure for us.

Mama was smart, courageous, and a hard worker. If she'd been given half a chance, she could have gone to school and done more with her life than just argue and fight with kids. I'm sure she loved us all, but how hard it must have been for a single woman back then to support and feed eight kids.

At Christmas time, some of the churches took pity on us and brought us clothes and food. I hated handouts even though we needed what they brought. It made me feel cheap and poor—like the trash of the world.

One year stands out for me as one of the worst. Mama didn't have any money that year, and the church brought us food and clothes as usual. My sister Carol and her husband were living with us, and they bought my twin sister and me a little tan purse for Christmas. Mama got something for the other kids, I think, but not for us because we had the stuff from the church and the purse that Carol had given us. I believe I wanted a doll that year, and when I didn't get it, or anything from Mama, I was hurt, and I cried.

If we said or did anything to hurt Mama, she wouldn't yell at us or discipline us, she would lay in her bed and cry. My disappointment hurt Mama that Christmas morning and she lay in her bed crying. I have no words for the guilt and pain I felt for hurting Mama. Even writing about it now makes my stomach knot and my throat constrict as if the breath in me cannot get out it hurts so bad. So, there we were—her crying in bed, and me crying from the disappointment of not getting that doll and the guilt I felt for hurting Mama. That was a Christmas I will never forget. It taught me that my pain wasn't allowed to exist if it caused her pain. Sobbing, I tried to tell her how sorry I was, but the damage was done, and most of that Christmas day was in ruins.

That was the pattern in our house, if you hurt Mama by being sad about something yourself, then the guilt of hurting Mama was much too difficult to bear. I tried hard to not hurt Mama, and I think that probably added to my Goody-Two-Shoes image.

Only as I write this have, I realized that I was taught by experience to bury my hurt and bury my anger and bury any feelings that would make Mama feel bad. I wonder how much I still do that today.

Don't Let Mama Know

Bury my hurt and bury my fear I cannot let it out.

I must not feel It must not be said this pain that I have.

The hurt may be real but bury it within.

If I let it out, then Mama will cry and my spirit will die.

What's worse to suffer? This gaping open hole inside my gut inside my womb, Or guilt at my Mama's tears?

My belly boils, threatens to spill over, hot saliva blisters its path through my breast it goes to rest, rising, constricts my throat, choked back, squeezed down push it down! push it down!

This flame might explode as the battle rages on; it wants to escape and must be detained.

If my tears break the dam, then Mama will see and this burning fire in my gut will be nothing to the ache in my soul that hurting Mama will bring.

Stem the tide, don't let go, maybe I'll run, maybe I'll scream, maybe I'll run inside and hide.

How selfish I am to hurt my Mama with these hot fumes steaming and searing inside of me.

Go away! go away! go away all! Wipe the tears off your face. Hide behind the lace. Don't let Mama trace these cries to you. Else she will weep and my heart will cry!

I just won't feel it; I just won't at all I will not listen to this roar in me!

I know, I'll just hide this pain away within Mama won't see it inside.

Mama never planned to raise us to hide our hurt and fear, she was just trying to get through her life and the pain of it all, but she taught me well, to hide my feelings inside.

Mama was diagnosed with Type I diabetes at age 38. She had heart disease, congestive heart failure, and some nerve damage from the diabetes. She always took numerous medications, always had her bottles of pills. She would find a doctor who'd give her one pill for one thing and then go to another for another kind of pill. I'm quite sure there were detrimental interactions between some of them, but there was no way you could tell Mama that.

One episode in particular shook our world and left us forever changed. I was still quite young, Mama had gone to work, and we were waiting for her to come home. She rode the bus to the end of our road and then walked about six blocks or so to our house. She didn't come home when we expected her and after waiting around for a time, someone got very nervous and started calling around, looking for her. All I remember is walking up and down the road looking for her—we didn't know what else to do. It was almost dark by the time we found her. She had experienced a drop in her blood sugar and had had a blackout, walking right past our place and out into some field with a ditch, where she'd fallen. We found her unconscious in the dirty ditch. We thought she was dead. Panic and chaos ensued as we called the ambulance to come get our Mama. Our world was rocked; we were scared to death, crying, as we waited to find out if she was dead. Those were some of the worst hours I have ever spent. In the hospital they were able to give her something to raise her blood sugar and bring her out of her blackout, so she came home to us again. But some damage was done; we forever lived in fear of losing our Mama after that.

During those years Mama met a couple of men she dated. Most did not want a woman with eight kids, so she was destined to spend most of her life alone. She met one man that she dated for years but he was married. She would meet him at his car at work and sit in his car and talk to him for hours on end. He never could bring himself to leave his wife, however, and eventually the relationship ended. He died a few years after that, supposedly a suicide, but Mama was always sure his wife had killed him.

Sometime later she met and dated another man who owned a grocery store in another small town in North Carolina. They married and we moved to this little town. I'm not sure who was happier—Mama or me. I was finally going to get a daddy; I would finally be like all the other kids and have a daddy who loved me. You have no idea how wonderful that sounded. I wonder what it is inside us that make us all want to be the same. By being the same, somehow, we think that makes us all right, but really it doesn't—we were never meant to be the same.

Anyway, we moved to the house behind the store, but before I could meet my "new daddy" the police came to the door. It seems our new daddy was married to not only Mama but to several other women as well. I never even got to meet my new daddy. Mama lay on the bed and cried, and I lay at the foot of the bed and cried even more—I'm not sure who was more upset —her or me. She went to the jail to see him and of course they got the marriage annulled. I think he went to jail but I have no idea.

That betrayal cut deep into both of us. For Mama, it was another man who had lied to her, used her, left her alone. For me, it shattered my dream of finally having a father and taught me early that the people you trust most can deceive you completely.

For a while, we stayed at the house with the store in front and ran the store, but it must not have made money because Mama closed it down after a while and we moved back up to the area that she knew best. Having access to what we called 'drinks' (our Southern term for soda pop) and candy was certainly something we had never had, and we sure enjoyed that part of the store. Probably the reason Mama couldn't make any money on the goods in the store was that we ate it all.

Our Southern summers were hot and muggy, but we had an ice cream truck that came around at least twice a week. Our next-door neighbors had little kids too, and they always got ice cream —and always teased us because we didn't. Many times, we ran into the house crying to Mama about being teased and asking her for ice cream. There were some occasions that she'd get mad at the neighbor children for teasing us, and even though we could ill afford to spend money on the ice cream man, on those occasions she would buy us all an ice cream.

As smart kids will do, we learned to manipulate the situation so that we got ice cream as often as possible. Children learn early how to survive, and we discovered that making Mama feel guilty about our differences from other kids could sometimes get us what we wanted. Poor Mama, no money and here we were figuring out a way to manipulate her into buying us ice cream. I might be able to laugh about this if Mama was still alive, and if I didn't feel so much guilt at adding to her already stressful life.

In later years, with most of her kids married or gone, Mama met a man who owned one of the houses she rented. He was single and had been for years. Mama really liked him and "set her cap for him." Remember, when our Mama set her mind to some-thing, she usually succeeded. She and Willoughby got married and for a short time, Mama seemed happy for the first time in

her life. She was able to go to the grocery store and buy whatever she wanted to eat, and to shop for whatever clothes she
wanted to wear. Neither were things that she had ever been able
to do before.

This period was the happiest I ever knew Mama to be. She was
good to him, and he was good to her. I was married by that time,
and into my own life, but we made a few trips back South to
visit her; it was such a peaceful thing to see her happy. Unfortunately, however, her happiness didn't last long. They'd been
married six years when Willoughby developed cancer and died.
Mama had another husband to bury. Once again, she was alone,
but at least she was better off financially than she had been
before, and she didn't have nine kids at home to feed.

CHAPTER 4

MY LIFE AS A TEEN BRIDE

I t's been weeks since I've written about my family and me. I've been busy—too busy to face this page, but tonight sleep won't come, and something calls to me. Each time I think I'm healed, that I've cried all the tears and felt all the pain, it erupts again like a volcano that simmers beneath the surface, then explodes with sudden fury that cannot be contained. I hide it for a while, then it bursts out—this need to write, this pull back to a time and place that shaped me. My body demands I finish this story before it can be free.

The writing wakes me Calls my name *Get up! Get up!*

Memories swim through my head, my heart, my soul, flowing through my blood, refusing to let me be whole.

My fingers know what to say, what to do.

My body remembers what needs telling even when my mind forgets.

Let my fingers glide—they think on their own, remembering what the writing wants While I try to hide inside.

Looking back to my years in the South, I had healed enough from my breakdown to live as a "normal girl" most of the time. But there were still periods when I became the watcher and the watched—sometimes it felt like the safest place to be. Years later, when my counselor told me there was no "normal," that normal was whatever normal meant for you, I thought *I wish I'd known that growing up.*

I felt sorry for the kids who got picked on, so I defended them, tried to make them feel better. But I also needed acceptance, and you didn't get accepted by befriending the underdogs. Caught between worlds—I was an underdog, but others had it worse, so I felt their pain while trying to gain acceptance myself. My solution: stay a little apart. It was safer.

At twelve, I started dating. After long days in the tobacco fields, feet aching like pins were stuck in them, legs hurting so bad I'd cry at night, my sisters and I would clean up, paint our faces, and walk down the dirt road to the corner store. We'd sit on the bench, waiting for boys to drive by—soldiers from Fort Bragg. Even at twelve, I never dated anyone younger than nineteen.

At twelve, I felt ancient, like I knew everything. I can't remember ever feeling young. Time would prove me incredibly wrong, but no one could have told me that then—not that anyone tried. Mama was so tired after working all day and worrying all night that she let us be. Too busy trying to feed us to track what we were doing, she made no rules. So, I made my own—set curfews, played gatekeeper for my sister and friend.

This old soul lived inside my young body, convinced she knew the "right" way, compelled to share that wisdom with my sisters.

The men I dated taught me lessons I wasn't ready for. One pinched behind my knees when I disobeyed—thank God for my brother-in-law who made him disappear. Another tattooed my name on his arm, then cut himself with a razor when I tried to break up. Then came the married man who took me to his house, raped me in his marital bed. Fear kept me going out with him; it always ended the same way, usually in his backseat. Eventually he vanished from my life—killed in Vietnam, I heard later. I never told anyone what he'd done, but I felt nothing but relief when I learned he'd died.

At fourteen, I met Mike. He seemed normal, kind, with parents, a real family. He didn't force himself on me or hurt me. After my experiences, he felt like salvation.

His family lived in Washington State, and when he described them, they sounded like everything I'd dreamed of. My world was spinning out of control. I kept putting myself in situations I couldn't handle, desperate for love but terrified I was becoming what others called me. When Mike asked me to marry him after a month of dating, I said yes.

Did I know what I was doing? Of course not. But something inside knew I needed escape—though I wouldn't let myself think it consciously.

I thought I knew everything—after all, I was fourteen, had been dating for two years, making my own rules, staying alive. God must have been watching over us because we easily could have met worse fates.

Sometimes I stayed with my brother and his wife, helping with their kids while they worked. He beat her; they fought, screamed, beat each other. I'd grab the children—one in my arms, one by the hand—and take them to the front yard, far enough that they couldn't hear the violence. So, when I married, I thought I'd seen everything, heard everything. How arrogant I was —to think life had no more lessons for me. But it's one thing to witness someone else's hell—it's another one to live it yourself. I'd simply traded one hell for another.

Mike was a heavy drinker—I realized later he'd been drunk most of our courtship. With no experience with alcohol, and since he mostly drank beer, I had no clue he was an alcoholic. It would be years before I even knew the term, understood the havoc of living with addiction.

The cycle began—drunk Mike was mean and nasty. Sober Mike was always sorry. Eighteen years of this pattern. His abuse was usually verbal, but there were physical moments— punching holes in our bed frame, throwing things, knocking over our Christmas tree. The year I was pregnant with my first daughter at sixteen, he literally tore our house apart. Nothing survived that night—not furniture, not peace, not my illusions.

He hit me a few times, but I told him: "Hit me again, and I'll wait until you're asleep and kill you with a butcher knife." He must have believed me. While he killed me with words, he rarely tried to hit me again.

Everything was my fault, he said. I was a whore, a slut. If I loved him enough—he wouldn't drink. If I gave him more sex, cooked breakfast more, made his lunch, became a better wife—then he wouldn't say cruel things, wouldn't drink, wouldn't destroy our home. He broke things, threw furniture, threatened me, and told me so often that his problems were my fault that I began believing him.

Our social outings ended the same way—him drunk, saying cruel things while I laid my head back to hide my tears from others. The next day brought apologies and promises—promises that lasted until the next time.

Eighteen years. Sometimes better, mostly worse. I could tell before he came home that tonight would be a drinking night. I'd see him drive through our small town and just know—tonight, he'll be drunk.

At his parents' house, he'd control himself until we reached our room. Then he'd rip off his shirt, buttons flying, and launch into his tirade about what a slut I was. My mother-in-law suggested I accept him, not argue, try this, try that. Church ministers said, "Love when there is no love. Show respect even when there is none." I tried everything. He still drank daily, still blamed me, and I remained that unloved little girl. The wonderful life I'd thought I was escaping to didn't exist—at least not here.

I thought about giving up many times, but giving up meant dying to me. I never really considered leaving—not for years. We separated two or three times but always reunited, probably because I didn't know how to be different. All my counseling said, "love even when you don't feel it." I'd turned to church, where I heard repeatedly that the man was head of household, deserving respect and love whether he earned it or not.

Many times, I thought about dying—taking enough aspirin to end it. I didn't know other methods, and since I never followed through, I must not have wanted it badly enough. I'm a survivor, a fighter, not a quitter. I got that from Mama—she had to be to raise nine kids alone.

We endured like this for years. I had four daughters, took care of them, made a life for us. To me, he was like having another child —one constantly out of control. He worked and earned money; I raised the kids. I finished high school through correspondence course (I'd quit in ninth grade to marry), took seminary courses, joined the PTA—doing everything to create a— "normal" family.

I tried venturing into the world—getting jobs, going to school— but each attempt threatened Mike, and when he felt threatened, the drinking and verbal abuse intensified. Church and school involvement were acceptable; anything else made me a whore in his eyes. Why would I want to be "out there" unless I was one?

Something inside always knew that continuing to push for independence would end the marriage. But I'd been taught marriage was forever, so leaving didn't seem like an option. We played this game: I'd try to have a life he deemed unacceptable; he'd drink and rage, and I'd quit and go home.

Then came the time when I was dying inside, smothering, couldn't breathe. I broke into a thousand jagged pieces. The crying wouldn't stop.

"No more" I said. "You have to stop."

He ripped the phone from the wall, grabbed a shotgun, threatened me with it, then turned it on himself. I took the girls and fled to his brother's house.

The next morning, he checked himself into treatment. They wanted to see me, but I was terrified. I was certain everything was my fault—his drinking, rage, abuse. If I'd loved him more, given him more sex, cooked breakfast, made lunch, been a better wife, then he'd be perfect. I always tried moving us away from his friends because *they* made him drink—never him. Most of all, I knew that if he stopped drinking, he'd be perfect, and we'd be perfect together.

I had no choice but to go to the treatment center. Terrified, expecting them to confirm how awful I was, how much I'd damaged him. But they didn't. They showed me a little girl hiding behind a door so she wouldn't hear her parents fighting. I started crying and couldn't stop for two days. I was that little girl —always hiding, always afraid.

Mike stayed a month in counseling while I saw my own counselor. He got out, but nothing changed. He'd quit drinking—not because of how much he'd hurt me or the kids, not because I couldn't stand it anymore. They convinced him he'd die if he didn't stop. All those years of my pain hadn't mattered. It was about him, always about him.

I thought things would improve, that I could live without fear, maybe take classes at community college. I signed up for pet psychology—it felt wonderful learning about something besides my pain. I thought he was well, that I was well, that I could stop being his mother.

He couldn't handle it. Unknown to me, he'd met another woman at the treatment center—a mother willing to play the role I no longer wanted.

He left me. We had cows and horses and four daughters, and he left. Took all the money, sold the hay for our animals, and vanished. After eighteen years, after everything I'd endured, he left me.

My stomach felt ripped out, like part of me had been cut away—leaving a gaping hole inside.

Then came shame—shame that I'd stayed, shame that he'd left me rather than me finding courage to leave him. Shame, pain, anger so hot it was a flame threatening to consume everyone in its path.

Then the fear took hold. How would I care for my daughters and myself? Pay bills? Buy food? Eighteen years later, I'd be poor again—a nobody with nothing, on welfare with four daughters to support. I'd run to the other end of the United States to escape being poor and invisible, and here I was again. The fear of being exactly where I started—like mother, like daughter. Alone with children and no way to survive.

Who is in the Mirror

I look in the mirror—who stares back at me? Is that me, Mama, or you staring back, laughing at me?

I'm so frightened, afraid to see who's looking back at me.

Pain lashes so deep it crushes me—crushes, cuts, smothers me. I can't breathe; I can't breathe.

The pressure holds me down, keeps me down, so far down I may never surface again.

Mama, I'm a little girl again, feeling pain, loss, fear, shame. I'm a nobody again.

I found a wonderful counselor—a godly, educated man who saw me weekly for a year. Determined never to end up with another alcoholic, I worked hard at growing up, becoming whole. I'd married so young I didn't know how to be complete. The Counselor gave his time because I couldn't afford to pay him—he helped me become whole and I slowly begin building a life for my girls and myself. I'll be eternally grateful to this man who took time to guide me through this phase. I think I paid him five dollars per visit. Can you imagine? Thank you, wherever you are, and thank you, God, for sending him.

After those initial months of feeling ripped apart—suddenly there was such intense freedom— I felt like a bird released from a cage. I could fly—soar to unknown heights— with no one to stop me. It was one of the most exhilarating times of my life.

Freedom

I was free— free to run and roam, young, alive, filled with hope to survive. I danced, I laughed, loved, cried.

I could soar to the sky, all-powerful, Be anything I wanted to be.

I celebrated, prayed, hurt, cried, but I was free.

The smothering lifted, the crushing gone. I'm alive! I'm alive!

I played, had fun, learned what it meant to be single again. I vowed never to be poor again, never to be unable to care for myself. So, I accelerated my life—eighteen years was a long time to make up.

At a Parents Without Partners dance, a man told me: "If you want to earn a man's salary, compete in a man's world. If you want a woman's salary, compete in a woman's world." I decided I wanted to compete in a man's world.

Writing this, I realize it's the first time I've thought about where my heart was in my career drive. I'd told my counselor I wanted to be a psychologist, but when this man spoke about money and taking care of myself and my kids, I listened. Hard to say if that was a mistake—it doesn't matter now, because that's what I did.

I studied, passed tests for my Production and Inventory Management certificate, then pursued a bachelor's in business administration. Working full-time, raising four girls, and attending school full-time—after all, I had to hurry, make up for eighteen years.

I found a nontraditional program where I could take bachelor-level courses while completing lower-division requirements through distance learning. Starting with twelve credit hours, needing ninety at lower division and ninety at bachelor's level, I worked on both simultaneously—usually four nights a week or two nights plus all weekend. In two years, I had my bachelor's. Sometimes driving home, I was so exhausted I didn't know where I was. But I was determined never to depend on anyone again.

I moved up in management, assuming happiness would follow. Not satisfied with a bachelor's, I completed my master's in business administration in the next two years. Obviously, my children suffered with me gone so much, but even in the suffering, they were happier and better off than when I was married to their father. While I'm proud of my accomplishments, I wish they hadn't come at my daughters' expense or been driven by fear.

Later, after Cliff, my husband now, came into our lives, my daughters experienced what a real father could be. They went from a dad who only spoke to them when he wanted help and otherwise ignored them, to a man who talked to them and listened. He took them to the zoo, carried my youngest on his shoulders, showed them patience and kindness. He didn't demand they help with farm work they were far too young to do. For the first time, they had a male figure who saw them as children to be cherished, not workers to be used.

I met Cliff at my first full time job after my divorce. I was feeling free and happy and ready to get going on some path that would help me support myself and my kids. I made $1497 a month and I was quite proud. It was far from enough to support us but that didn't stop me from being excited and proud. Mike paid $100 per month per child so I got $400 a month and no alimony. I hadn't had any idea what I was doing with the divorce so we were left with far too little to live on as I would find out the hard way. I laugh now at how naïve I was but never having earned money for any length of time I was proud that I could get a job and earn my own money.

On the job I worked hard and tried to learn everything I could. I found I liked working and getting to know people at work, including Cliff. Quiet and kind, he listened as I rambled about life. We'd spend time after work standing in the parking lot, talking. We became friends first—he was the first person I thought of when something new happened, always ready to laugh with me or offer advice.

After months of friendship, we began dating. One day we drove to Cannon Beach. After walking barefoot in the warm sand, I struggled to put my shoes back on—sand stuck all over the bottoms of my feet. Cliff had me sit on a bench, then knelt and gently brushed the sand from my feet before putting my shoes on for me.

It was the most loving thing anyone had ever done for me.

In that moment, I understood what tenderness looked like. Not grand gestures or passionate declarations, but this—someone caring for me without expecting anything in return, seeing my small struggle and simply helping. After years of being told I was worthless, here was a man treating me like I mattered, like I deserved gentle care.

With Mike, I'd felt like I had another child to take care of—one constantly out of control, demanding attention, creating chaos. With Cliff, I had an adult I could talk with about all things in life. Real conversations about ideas, dreams, problems, solutions.

He didn't need me to manage his emotions or clean up his messes. He was a partner, not another burden.

We'd date for years before our relationship deepened. I had barriers up, determined never to let anyone hurt me again. While I quickly grew to love him, I didn't want to surrender my newfound freedom or self.

It took me a long time to realize that true love means wanting the best for the other person—not being so insecure you don't want your partner to grow or experience life fully. After many years, I finally understood: two halves don't make a whole in a relationship, but two wholes make something truly beautiful.

CHAPTER 5
THE SOUTH CALLS ME HOME

I've been running my entire life. Running from the South, from my family, from my body that stores pain like a vault. Running from poverty and bad marriages, from shame I carry inside no matter how hard I try to hide it—even from myself. It's time to stop running, and I hope I can.

But there were happy times too—visits home to see my sisters and Mama after we'd all grown up and married. Those visits hold some of my happiest family memories.

Mama always had impossibly small bathrooms—just big enough for an old round white porcelain sink with no cabinet, a small bathtub, and the toilet. So cramped you could barely turn around, certainly not designed for more than one person.

But whenever we visited—sisters from out of town joining those who'd stayed local—we'd decide to go shopping, which meant getting ready together. Four, sometimes five of us would cram into that tiny bathroom, putting on makeup and talking. Our tiny bathroom became our sanctuary—the place to share things that hurt us and made us cry, silly things like makeup tips and hair advice, stories about each other and childhood escapades. Sometimes we laughed until we cried; other times we bared our souls. Always in that suffocating little room.

I have no idea how we all fit, but we did. When we emerged—sometimes two hours later—we'd be drenched in sweat. The husbands, of course, had been yelling and pounding on the door the entire time, convinced we were talking about them. Since there was usually trouble with one husband or another, they were probably right.

I can still hear Bertha's husband Joe calling, "Bert! Bert, aren't you ready yet? Come on, Bert, we're going to be late!"

Or Carol's husband Jimmy: "Carol! Carol, honey, let's go. It's time to go, Carol!"

They were funny to listen to—they just couldn't stand that we were in there and they didn't know what we were saying. The husbands always worried about what their wives might be telling about them, which we found hilarious because our time wasn't spent on them for the most part.

Bert would emerge laughing, even her eyes smiling as she wiped sweat from her face with the tissue she always carried in her right hand—the one missing a thumb. Heavyset most of her adult life, she was constantly perspiring in the Southern heat and humidity.

Carol would come bopping out with a laugh that seemed to erupt from the bottom of her feet and roll out in a cackle, then pop her hand over her mouth to contain it. Somewhere along the way, she'd convinced herself she was the ugly duckling brought to life. With her red hair, freckles, and big teeth, I'm sure she'd been teased enough to believe it. A crossed eye meant you never knew who she was looking at when she spoke. She was beautiful, but you could never convince her of that.

The nieces and nephews still living in North Carolina talk about those days when their mothers spent half the day in the bathroom. We had so much fun in those tiny spaces.

But only now, as I write this, do I realize what I never shared in that sacred space. I never told my sisters or Mama about Mike—how much he drank, how verbally abusive he became, how his cruelty was always "my fault" for not making his lunches or not having enough sex with him. I never described how he'd act almost normal around other people, then transform behind closed doors into a monster who'd rip off his shirt, reeking of spoiled alcohol, telling me what an awful person I was. How I'd try to hide my tears by resting my head on the back of my chair during his drunken rant. How he threw things, broke things and punched holes in our bed's headboard.

I'm not sure most of them ever knew about the verbal or physical abuse. Why didn't I tell them? Maybe I believed it was all my fault and didn't want them to know. Maybe I just wanted to enjoy my time with them. Maybe I thought this was normal based on what I'd witnessed in my own family growing up. Its such a shame I didn't talk to someone who might have helped me see the truth sooner.

As I write this, I feel overwhelmed. How can I complete this book? There are still so many to write about—so many who died, who hurt too much for one family to endure. Maybe it's important for my healing. Maybe it needs saying for my children. Maybe, after everything, it doesn't matter. I don't know, but I'll try to finish this story.

The feeling washes over me: I must go home this year. One more trip back to the South, back to my roots. I must see their graves: Daddy, Mama, Jr, Bertha, Carol, and my Twin Berline; see where they lived and died. The South calls to me—honeysuckle trees, that distinctive smell, sun streaming through tall pines. It whispers: *Come home, just for a while, come home.* I must find a way. The South has something to say to me, and I need to discover what it is.

The South's Song
Southern breeze blows, Southern sun glows, sweet honeysuckle tell bittersweet truths.

The South calls my name, blows the same refrain: You need to come—we have something to say.

This South in you no longer at bay.

Some things you must learn, or maybe just feel.
You must come home to be real, must come home to heal.

Walk the ground of your youth, walk the sand your Mama did.
Feel earth beneath bare feet, feel sand and sun tickle your toes.

See yourself in youth and pain, see your sisters home again.

Feel the pain, feel the shame of who you were and who you are.

I must face this part of me—this part *is* who I am.
I can run, but I cannot hide from the truth inside.

I'm who I am, and the shattered pieces must be joined.

The broken me must go home to become one, not two or three.
To be one and not more—there is much work to do.

The message is clear. Integration requires facing everything—
not just the parts I can bear to remember, but the whole truth.
The South holds pieces of me I left behind, and I cannot be
whole until I reclaim them. The journey home isn't just
geographical; it's spiritual, psychological, essential.

I will go home. I will walk that ground, breathe that air, feel that
earth beneath my feet. I will gather the scattered pieces of
myself and, finally, become one.

CHAPTER 6
DADDY'S FACE ON MY TWIN

After my divorce, Berline—my twin sister—started getting horribly sick. She'd developed Type I diabetes in her early twenties, and the disease had ravaged her body, stolen her sight and was destroying her kidneys. A damaged heart valve, the legacy of scarlet or rheumatic fever from childhood, now threatened her life. She needed open-heart surgery to survive what had already become a living hell on earth.

Though all my sisters were struggling with illness, Berline was the most critical—or so it seemed then.

I flew home to see her as often as I could afford, as often as I could bear. Going home was like walking barefoot over hot coals —so painful you jumped from one to the next seeking relief, only to find each new coal hotter and more searing than the last.

Divorced with four daughters to support alone, I was living my own private hell, most of my time consumed by simple survival.

But when Berline went to Duke University Hospital for heart surgery, I flew down to be with her.

When I reached the hospital, she was sleeping. I looked down at her face, and I knew.

As I watched Berline lying there, unconscious from surgery, my mind drifted back to the little bench near the corner store on the dirt road where we grew up. It was there we'd decided we hated our names and needed new ones. She chose Lynn; I chose Jean. We were maybe twelve or fourteen—too young to know who we were, old enough to want to be someone different. She let Lynn go after a few years, settling back into Berline. I kept Jean, especially once I started traveling with my Army husband. Looking back, it was childlike and a little silly, but it was ours—a tiny rebellion, a moment of imagining a different life.

You do have to wonder what twin girls that young were doing on a bench waiting to meet guys. Clearly, we had no business being out there at all.

So many thoughts flood your mind when you're sitting, waiting, hoping the person you love will wake up and be okay. Many years have passed now, and the pain is just as deep as it was that day in the hospital.

I See Death
She was lying there, her face dark and bare.

It was her face but not her there— Daddy, Daddy's face instead.

I looked at her face but saw his face, and knew that in spite of it all death had come back on us to call.

I was a child when death stole Daddy from us all—Daddy's face I saw, strong and silent in his dark blue suit, lying in his silk-white coffin, his face dark, drained of life.

Now death visits again. Rather than Daddy, it is my other, my all, my twin sister, myself, on whom he has come to call.

I didn't understand how I could know, but there was no doubt inside me—Berline was going to die. I wasn't sure when, but I knew she didn't have long. My insides felt open exposed filled with crushing pain that was like a physical attack crushing me from the inside out as I tried to hide this terrible knowledge and simply be present when she woke.

Watching Berline struggle to live each day was like a raging inferno that burned from the inside out made worse because I could not allow it to seek any relief. I needed to be present for her. I stayed until her surgery was over and she was out of immediate danger, then—with a job and four young children waiting—I flew home.

Each day we thought might be her last. I would walk, run, then walk again, praying desperately: *Please God, take this away. Please help her today—not to have pain, just for today.*

She was my twin, my other half, the one who'd shared a womb with me, who'd sat on that park bench and chosen a new name, who'd crammed into tiny bathrooms with our sisters. We'd survived tobacco fields and poverty, dysfunction and abuse, only for this—her body betraying her when she'd finally found some peace.

Being so far away felt like torture. Every phone call might bring the news I dreaded. Every day that passed without word felt like borrowed time. Part of me was dying with her, and I was powerless to stop it from three thousand miles away.

My prayers changed from requests for healing to pleas for mercy—not for a miracle, but for an end to her suffering. When you love someone that much, sometimes letting go becomes the only kindness left to offer.

I had seen death's face before, in Daddy's coffin when I was too young to understand its permanence. Now I recognized it again, wearing my sister's features, and I understood exactly what it meant. Death wasn't finished with our family. It had more visits to make, more lives to claim, more hearts to break.

All I could do was wait, pray for her peace, and prepare myself for a loss that would tear away half of who I was. My twin, my mirror, my other self—soon to be just a memory held in a heart that would never again feel complete.

CHAPTER 7
DEATH COMES FOR MY MAMA

I'd been home from seeing Berline only a couple of days when my sister Ruth called to tell me Mama was sick and in the hospital. This wasn't unusual. Mama frequently had low blood sugar episodes that would cause her to lose consciousness, landing her in the hospital where they'd give her something to bring her out of the coma. As bad as it sounded, I thought this was one of those times, that it would be like all the others—she'd be all right.

I felt so war-torn, like I couldn't handle any more pain right then, so I didn't call for a couple of days. Then something happened: she fell, couldn't talk, and something had gone horribly wrong. This wasn't the usual hospital stay for Mama after all.

My Sister Ruth called: "You need to come."

Death Comes for Mama

I got that dreaded call: You need to come, you cannot run.

Mama has fallen—the family we are calling.

You need to come, do not be late.

Mama needs you, do not wait.

Mama, Mama of mine, do not leave me behind.

Wait, Mama! Wait for me—wait for me to see you one more time, wait for me to say goodbye.

I arrived too late. Mama was ready to go to see my Daddy, her mate.

My brother James, sister Roma, and I lived within hours of each other, so we flew home together. We reached the hospital only to find Mama in a coma—they didn't expect her to revive. The doctors said there was nothing to be done. We pushed him. He said there might be a slim possibility of life if he operated, but although she might live, he couldn't guarantee in what condition. He didn't recommend surgery.

We waited and waited while pain and pressure built.

Ruth had been with Mama since admission. She was certain Mama wanted to go home to die and was adamantly against any medication. We were all at the hospital, the mood near hysteria. Ruth was in obvious physical and mental pain.

"Mama does not need medication," Ruth declared. "God will heal her. All she has to do is name it and claim it, and God will heal her."

We were exhausted and anxious—someone needed to respond, and an argument erupted about whether Mama should have morphine for her pain.

The doctor was with us. "Your mother will be more comfortable on morphine, but it will slow her body functions."

"What does that mean?" I asked.

"If we put her on morphine, we're just trying to make her comfortable until she dies."

"How long does she have?"

"We don't know. Could be days, or she could stay in a coma for weeks and need to be moved to another facility."

"Oh no," I gasped.

Ruth panicked because we were discussing this in front of Mama.

"No!" she almost screamed. "We do not need to talk about this now, and certainly not in front of Mama!"

I knew she was right and felt ashamed for not getting the doctor out of Mama's room first. But I also knew Mama was in pain, and as much as I wanted to believe all she needed was to "claim healing," I didn't believe healing would happen. My other sisters were there, and somehow, we all decided Mama should be put on morphine. We didn't want her in pain.

Ruth seemed beaten somehow and went home that night. Days moved into a week with Mama on morphine. We took turns staying with her.

My oldest sister Bertha and I were in the waiting room.

"Bert," I said, "I think I should go home."

"What are you talking about?" she asked.

"I feel useless. It seems like I'm not helping anyone by being here. Maybe I should just go home."

"How can you say that?" She was almost crying. "Of course you're helping us. Of course we need you here."

As we hugged, I promised to stay.

Tension mounted, tempers flared—everyone went a little mad. Ruth wanted to take Mama home to die. Roma was emotionally unstable, so we called her husband to fly down and help control her and the situation. When her diabetes is out of control, it rages, and Roma rages with it. One morning she slapped James when he touched her arm trying to calm her down.

I wasn't there and didn't understand why she'd hit him. Only recently did I learn she was trying to get us to listen, to understand that by not giving Mama pain medication, we were hurting her. Now I understand her frustration—she was trying to tell us what was happening, that we shouldn't listen to Ruth's rigid beliefs about no medication, but we weren't hearing her. She grew more frustrated with us.

I understand now, but then it was just one more crisis to manage. It was such a scene that nurses threatened to kick us all out. I talked with them; my sisters talked with them. We agreed to only two visitors at a time. We were in a horror movie, but we *were* the horror movie.

The first week became the second as we took turns staying nights. One evening, Bertha, Carol, and I decided to stay together. It was strange—we were in such pain, but Bertha lay on one bed, Carol on the chair bed they'd brought, and I stretched across a chair, periodically joining one of them on the bed.

We talked of old times, laughed about things Mama used to do— what she was like, how mad she could get, all the little joys in our lives. It was like old times when we'd gather and talk and laugh as Mama sat on the sidelines, just happy to be there with us, listening.

Except this time was horribly different, it would never be the same again. Oh my Lord, how I miss them—how hard it is not to have them to talk to, to laugh with, to just call once in a while. Dear God, will the tears and pain never be gone?

We talked and laughed with Mama there in bed beside us—she seemed to know we were there. I hope she heard us and just enjoyed listening, as she had so often when I'd visit and she'd cook all day, having the table full of food when I walked in. I'd call ahead of time and tell her all the things that she and my sisters made that I wanted to eat when I got there and they would have it all laid out on the table when I would walk in from the airport. There were biscuits, chicken and dumplings, fried chicken, pound cake, coconut cake, black eyed peas and lots of things I can't even remember. Those were such fun times, sitting and talking all day and the evening. The table would stay full as one group of visitors followed another, as we sisters and brothers sat and talked and laughed.

Ruth kept insisting we take Mama home to die. It was decided we would get together to discuss it. We sat in a circle in my brother Roman's big upholstery shop like we were holding a board meeting about life and death, but none of us knew the rules. Our oldest brother Roman, who'd always been the elder with the final say, sat slumped in his chair and didn't have much to contribute. I couldn't fathom taking Mama home. How would we care for her? Keep her out of pain? What were they thinking? Mama, who would take pills like candy, would certainly want whatever she needed to manage pain. I've never understood that meeting or its purpose.

Ruth was adamant that Mama had said she wanted to go home to die, her voice getting higher and more insistent with each repetition. "She told me, she told me she wanted to die at home!"

Carol cried and said many things that seemed to tumble out in no order—something about Mama's kitchen, about how she'd always been there, about who would take care of the house. I couldn't understand what she even wanted after she finished talking. She was the sister who'd always lived close to Mama, probably saw her daily, would stop by for dinner or coffee, was always there with Mama and probably knew her best as an adult. But grief had scrambled her words into fragments.

Bertha just cried, dabbing at her eyes with tissues that kept shredding in her hands. For the first time in my life, watching her, I realized how shy she was. She'd nod when someone spoke to her directly, but mostly she just wept quietly. I wondered how I could have missed that all those years—why wouldn't I have known how shy she was, how she'd laugh with us but not have much to say? She was so broken up I couldn't tell what she wanted either.

Roma had worked for doctors most of her working life, knew medical terms and understood the ramifications of this kind of move better than the rest of us. She sat straighter than the rest of us, speaking in clipped, practical sentences: "You can't manage IV morphine at home. You can't handle a coma patient. What if she stops breathing?" She was calmer but equally adamant that Mama should not come home.

Everyone talked over each other—Ruth's voice rising with religious conviction, Carol's words dissolving into sobs, Roma stating medical facts that no one wanted to hear, Bertha crying quietly, Roman staring at his hands. **"The madness of it"** We were like broken toys, each making our own noise but none of us working properly anymore.

When my turn came, I cut through the chaos: "Mama will not go home. If I need to, I'll take it to court. Mama needs to be in the hospital." The room went quiet except for Carol's sniffling and the hum of fluorescent lights overhead. We all stared at each other like we'd just woken up from the same nightmare and weren't sure what was real. I found it interesting that it was me, certainly not the daughter who had lived there or been there that in this instance I became the one who knew what to do and the rest of the family listened to me. I have marveled at that knowledge many times since then.

I don't know what stopped the meeting or who made what decision, but it finally ended, and we all drifted away. Regardless of the outcome, the meeting worked off some steam. I went to the hospital to spend the night with Mama. James and Roma were supposed to relieve me in the morning.

Morning came. Mama hadn't rested much through the night. James and Roma didn't come—their relief time came and went. I was exhausted from being awake all night, so I called to find everyone was sleeping in. Berline called to say she was sleeping in a little and would be there soon.

I was alone with Mama.

The moment of dying

Something was happening to Mama. I didn't understand—she wasn't breathing right, something was wrong. *Oh my God, what was I to do?* Frantic, I called the nurse.

I stood next to the bed, afraid to breathe, afraid to move, to say anything.

"Talk to her," the nurse said. "Hold her hand. Tell her it's okay."

My final gift to her

"Mama, it's okay," I whispered, holding her hand. "You don't have to worry anymore. It's okay to let go, Mama. Don't worry. You can let go. Go see Daddy and Willoughby. Be peaceful, Mama. Tell Daddy hello for me."

With tears streaming down my face, I let her go.

Her breathing was ragged, then shallow, then just quiet—like a bird that's gone to sleep on its perch. Mama was gone. My Mama was gone. The pain raged inside me; my Mama was gone. Mama was only 67 when she died.

The nurse asked me to step outside. I stood in the hall, brain dull with pain, not knowing what to do. Then I saw her—my blind twin sister being led down the hall by her husband to Mama's room.

Oh my God, I panicked. *What will she do? What will she say? Will this be the last straw? Will she die today as well?* My eyes darted around, looking for help, pleading with the nurses to help me tell my twin sister that our mother was dead, that she was too late, that Mama was gone. My stomach hurt, my chest was tight. I felt like I might explode.

I can't run, I thought, *but oh God, I wanted to run. Okay,* I told myself, *you must be strong. You have to hold up, help your sister. You can do this. Breathe. You can do this.*

She dropped into the chair outside Mama's room when I told her Mama was gone. I knelt beside her to comfort her, wrapping my arms around her as she talked while my mind whirled on. Oh, how I hated that day! *My God, my God, why have you forsaken us? Why is this deadly strain, this deadly disease part of us? Why, Lord, why?*

"I was so tired from last night, I slept in," Berline cried. "If I had just gotten up a little earlier, I could have been here."

Tears streamed down both our faces.

My sister who could not see, who was in so much pain that every breath was an effort, now had not only our Mama's death to bear but the fact that she hadn't gotten to the hospital in time. My chest felt like it would cave in from the pain of it all.

"Did she die with a flutter like a little bird?" she asked.

"Yes," I answered in surprise. "She did."

"I was with Donnie's mama when she died, and that's how she died," she continued. "I want to go in with her for a few minutes."

Don and I led her to Mama's body, where she held her hand and cried. She was so strong, much stronger than I'd imagined. Berline handled it—she did not die that day. Not that day. She went home while I waited for other family members to come. It felt like the day would never end.

Bertha and Carol fell apart. Ruth was so torn up she was in a daze—she'd never really expected Mama to die. For all her prayers and belief, she truly thought Mama would live. She felt like she'd somehow failed.

I thought Bertha might have a heart attack herself. My brother Gaston stayed home, wouldn't come to the hospital. My older brother Roman, the patriarch, was so broken up he didn't have much to say. His wife Gaynell made the funeral arrangements. I knew then why it had been important for me to stay. I had been needed after all.

Years before, to the horror of all her children—me included—Mama had not only picked out and paid for her coffin but had laid down in it to make sure it was comfortable. Our Mama, always thinking ahead. When she'd done it and told us, we'd all had a fit, then laughed and talked about her lying in her coffin to make sure it fit. Now we were glad she had—glad she'd picked what she wanted. She'd decided to be buried next to

Willoughby instead of Daddy. She'd even made her funeral arrangements easy for us.

I stayed with my twin sister Berline while funeral arrangements were made. Our sister-in-law did all the planning—all we had to do was agree. We were so thankful for her. Mama was placed in the funeral home for private family viewing. It was just her body, not her there, but I couldn't bring myself to look at her.

Then the night before burial came the viewing for extended family and friends—Southern custom, at least in the South we knew.

My beautiful twin sister, so elegant and poised, sat in the front row of the church. You would have thought she was hosting a dinner party as she graciously greeted each person, smiling and telling them how glad she was they'd come. She stayed the entire night—a Southern belle to the end was my twin sister, Berline. This woman, so wracked with pain herself, was the most gracious and beautiful person I've ever seen. I was so proud of her.

At the funeral service the next day, I remember thinking: *Here we all are, Mama and Daddy's children, here to bury another parent.* Mama had a hard life with us, but no matter—we'd all stuck together. She could have walked away and left us, she could have put us in a foster home, but instead she did the hard work, the pain, the hardship of raising nine kids on your own. Here we were for the world to see that our Mama had managed to keep us together after all, to raise us. Now we all had families of our own, and somehow that made us—and most of all her—successful. She'd done it, but now she was gone.

Berline and I went to Mama's house to take a few things before I left town—a few things to remember Mama by, as if a thing, an inanimate object, would ever be needed to remember our Mama.

I took a wooden pastry bowl that Mama had always used to mix her Southern biscuits and pastry. ("Pastry," for those who don't know, isn't sweets but what you might call dumplings in our South, though somewhat different.) Biscuits and pastry was always my favorite meal with Mama—the required food when I came to town. Weeks before visits, I'd call Mama and Bertha with my "list" of foods to have ready.

Mama had made some quilts by hand in the years before her death, before Berline lost her sight. We took a couple of quilts and other things, going through them that night at Berline's home. It would have been funny if it hadn't been so tragic. Berline sat beside me on her sofa while I explained each item we took from our box. We'd take an item out, talk about it, decide who was going to take it and then review the next item.

We took out the quilts—Berline took one, then I was to take one. I described it to her, and as she sat gazing ahead with blind eyes, I could tell memories were flooding back. This was a quilt she and Mama had worked on together. How could I take it? I gave it to her. There were several more items that held special memories for Berline, so I let her take them, more concerned that she be happy than that I take anything. These quilts were just a representation of the losses I incurred by moving away and not enjoying those years of special times with my Mama.

She had stayed; I had moved away. She had more memories of Mama than I did. I've questioned that decision many times and realized all the memories I lost by not living close to my Mama and sisters. A visit every year or so is never enough time to make all the memories you want. My fear and hatred of my life growing up in the South had always been such a part of me that it kept me from returning to live there. I needed to be somewhere else where I could be someone else, not the person who'd grown up in the South.

It was over, as over as it ever gets. I flew home. In my own bed, I could smell death, taste it, like I'd been in dying fields—restless dreams of dying and death. It felt overwhelming, it seemed to live in my head, my heart, my breath, my smell, it consumed me. I couldn't get away from it. It was me and I was it.

"Is there a God?" I screamed in my head. "Is this all there is to life? What has all this been for? How can we be here and then just be no more?"

I'd been a Christian for years, but now I didn't know. "Do I really believe? Is God there? Is there really life after death?"

My heart, soul, and mind screamed with the pain of unanswered questions. I was changed, forever changed. In my head, everything that had happened in those two weeks at the hospital had to flow through my subconscious to form one mind. I dreamed of it, all of it step by step. I was no longer the same person, nor would I ever be.

I didn't understand how everyone could walk around acting as if the world was the same when my Mama had died, my twin was in brutal pain, my world had changed but no one else seemed to notice or care. I couldn't get the smell and feel of death off me. I couldn't sleep. I had to run.

Run and hide
Run and hide, run and hide little girl, when life's too hard, run and hide.

Mama died-run and hide.

I know the thing: go buy a ring.

After all, what does it matter? All the struggle, all the strife—What's it for?

Do what you want, buy what you wish, grab life before the death rattle wins the battle.

Who cares for career and more? My Mama died!

The ring no magic thing

I bought a ring, a pretty amethyst, shiny, sparkly thing. It glittered and glowed, in the sun it swayed and swirled.

My ring and I, we ran and walked, cried and talked.

The ring a perfect thing but not a magic scene, no lasting peace to bring.

Mama was gone, but my pain lived on. After a while it subsided —or maybe I just learned to live with it better and wasn't so surprised to find that for others, their world was unchanged. Besides, there was no more time to feel—there were kids to feed, a job to attend, and school. And then there were the others who were sick and dying.

I pushed it inside to hide once again.

CHAPTER 8
HALF OF ME MISSING

Berline and I were fraternal twins, not identical, and she was older by a whopping ten minutes. She had dark hair, dark complexion, and looked like Daddy. I was taller, fair-skinned with red hair, and favored Mama. We looked less like each other than we did some of our other sisters. Though I was shy and unsure, I hid it with talking while she was naturally quieter. I always felt she was prettier—as kids, I envied her because she didn't get teased for having red hair like I did.

The Twin Bond

She and I so different yet so alike—a part of me from conception, a part of my heart.

We lived very different, separate lives, but if one thought, the other called.

Close but not—a wall stood between, a wall I never understood, too big to move.

Maybe afraid of what the other knew, where there were no shades or blinds to hide.

The memory of her still a part of me—and not just me, but the body of me.

Her breath, my breath. Her fears, my fears. Our bodies as one.

My body remembers her inside the womb, now inside her tomb.

Though we both had tempers, I was more afraid of "letting mine loose," while she would fight with abandon. I always thought she was prettier, nicer, more genteel—a proper Southern lady—while I was the outspoken, brash one. In my mind, she was the strong one, willing to try almost anything, while I held back, afraid. The fights scared me—that total abandon, the out-of-control rage—so I always backed down.

She was the one who, when we were older and running around the neighborhood on our own, decided we needed to walk over the train trestle high above the Cape Fear River. That was the night we got picked up by police and brought home to Mama to explain why we were out that late, walking over the trestle.

When we started dating at twelve, we'd find places to hang out and meet boys—like Fayetteville, the military town within walking distance, where men would try to pick you up. She was always game to go; I was always trying to persuade her not to get in cars with strangers. But no matter what I said, she was determined to go, so I'd go along.

One experience sticks in my mind: we let a couple of guys pick us up one night walking home from downtown Fayetteville.

We'd been out with them for hours and wanted to go home, but they wouldn't take us. We were scared to death. Finally, when we promised we'd see them the next night, they took us home. You can bet we didn't go out with them again! We told Carol's husband Jimmy, an Army soldier then, and when the guys came to get us, Jimmy read them the riot act and threatened to call the police. We were so grateful to him that night.

Several similar episodes occurred where we put ourselves in grave danger—it's a wonder we got by as unscathed as we did.

It seemed I took on the moral conscience of the two of us when it came to dating and running around. I'm not sure how or why it developed, but that's who I was during our growing-up years. It probably stems back to the little girl trying so hard to be good so she'd be loved and accepted.

It seemed we were always moving—I'm not sure we ever stayed in the same school district more than a year. Mama would find a new place and off we'd go, staying in the same general area but moving just far enough to mean new schools and new friends.

In one neighborhood where we lived, siblings Berline, Ruth, James, and I walked to school. During our walk, we'd pass a house under construction with a hole in the backyard—probably for the septic system. Many times, my brother and sisters would decide to skip school and hide in that hole. Being the one always afraid of getting caught, I'd go to school while they stayed in that hole all day. Another example of why I was called "Goody-Two-Shoes" throughout childhood.

Besides being afraid of getting caught, I loved school. While I didn't like how we were treated, I loved learning about new and better things. I'd leave school in the afternoon, let them know it was time to go home, and off we'd go. I never could figure out what they did in that hole all day, but I certainly didn't want to be in it with them. As you can imagine, when I felt it was my duty to tell Mama about the hole, I didn't endear myself to them.

No matter what we did in those years, we were always together. We might have a couple of other friends here and there, but we did everything together—we had an unbreakable bond. I didn't realize how deep this bond was until years later. Even with this special connection, we still fought like all siblings.

When we were teens, Berline and I were fighting at the top of stairs in some welfare-housing apartment we lived in. She ended up pushing me down the stairs, broke my front tooth, and killed the root. The tooth turned dark, and I lived with it until I was in my thirties and divorced. I finally had a crown put on after about twenty years of having a dark front tooth. You might wonder why I didn't get it taken care of after I married. Of course, Mama wouldn't have had money for a dentist, but you'd think I would have gone after marriage. Oh well, such is life, as they say.

As kids, whenever our brother—three years younger—teased Berline or made her mad, she'd go after him with a butcher knife. Many times, she chased him up a tree, knife in hand. So funny now, but of course it wasn't then.

I remember how our family's strong emotions almost frightened me. Somewhere inside, I learned I had to keep myself under control because if I gave in, my temper would totally overtake me and there was no telling what I might do. Berline had that fighting spirit, yet she was shy and spoke softly with that long Southern drawl.

At one point in our youth, Berline ran away from home. Hard as I try, I cannot remember why. I just remember Mama driving that old gray Buick all over town, up and down every street, with me in the backseat straining my eyes to find Berline amid the busy Army town.

We found her three days later in the crowded train station where soldiers and civilians were coming and going. I still have no idea why she ran away. I think there was a lot bottled up in her that we never talked about, even as adults. Maybe if I'd lived closer, we would have had time to talk and share stories of our youth—why we did the things we did and became the women we were to become. As it was, we never got that time.

I was first to marry at fourteen; she followed months later. We got together often while I still lived in North Carolina, but my husband was in the Army, so we started moving around a lot. Berline and I grew apart to some extent—the apart that happens when you don't live close enough to see each other often.

As I write this, it strikes me how much I value my relationship with my daughters and remaining sisters and brothers. I know this is because I've felt the stark reality of losing family, each before their time, leaving so quickly and harshly.

However, during those years, I was glad to be far away from the place I blamed for all the pain hidden in my heart. It was this pain and hurt that drove me all these years. They say what stays hidden inside is what drives your behavior, and I can certainly attest to that.

It seemed Don, Berline's husband, wanted her to stay away from her side of the family, so for years her involvement was minimal. He also seemed to make all the family decisions, and knowing Berline's personality, I never really understood that. She wouldn't even get gas in the car unless he'd said to do it.

"Berline," I'd say, "your gas tank is almost empty. Shouldn't we stop and get gas?"

"Well," she'd drawl in her slow, Southern, let's-take-forever-to-get-anything-out voice, "guess I better ask Donnie."

The rest of us used to kid about how it could take five minutes for Berline to get one sentence out. Her mother-in-law lived with them for years, and since she spoke even more Southern and slower than Berline, we blamed her for our sister's slow manner of speaking—holding onto each word as if letting it go too soon would be unladylike. "Slow as molasses," we'd say about her talking or making any decision.

She always had to ask Donnie first. We laughed about how she'd never do anything unless she asked Donnie, and how it took her forever to finish a sentence but let someone mess with her boys and she was right there, ready to beat them up. There seemed to be two people inside her, and they didn't match up. I never understood what made her so dependent on him when she was so independent. She was very private, and I wasn't around all those years, so I never asked why. I believe there was something in her that was wild and free, but she hid it away.

Berline had three sons, and as kids do, they were often in fights with neighbor kids. There were many stories of occasions when she went to the neighbors' mothers if she felt her boys had been taken advantage of. A few times she got into fights with the mothers themselves. I heard she slapped one and threatened more than one. This small, soft-spoken woman was a fighter, and everyone knew it.

In her early twenties, Berline developed Type 1 diabetes and had to immediately start insulin injections. They also found a defective heart valve around the time she started having children and warned her she might one day need heart surgery. She put it off for years—either the doctors never impressed her with any urgency, or she just couldn't face it.

It was after the diabetes progressed to blindness and the disease attacked her body in numerous ways that the operation became imperative. She underwent heart surgery about one year before Mama died. Mama had said she couldn't bear for one of her kids to die before she did. As it happened, none did, but several followed quickly behind her.

Berline was in the throes of her illness when Mama died, continuing her battle with diabetes and heart disease over the next year. She had several laser surgeries attempting to regain her eyesight. As diabetes progressed, she lost kidney function and had to go on dialysis—twice a week at a clinic, spending hours on the machine to rid her body of waste.

Her body was failing in every way. She spent most time in bed, so sick that her hours were torture. Don would make her breakfast, help her eat, then go to work, only to rush home at midday to check on her and prepare lunch. Then he'd drive twenty minutes back to work, only to return at night for the same ritual. This was their daily routine for a year or more. Berline struggled to get her body well, going to many specialists, doing everything she could to make her body whole.

During the more than two years she was so sick, I flew home several times to see her. I knew each time I left might be the last time I'd see her, so leaving was torture—but seeing her in pain was torture too. There seemed no way out of the pain.

I remember the last time I left—she and Don took me to the airport. Even though she was blind, I could tell she watched me leave and wanted me to stay. I still feel tremendous guilt that I didn't just put my life on hold and go back to North Carolina to be with her. Now it seems like, what would it have hurt to do that for a year? At the time, it didn't seem like I could.

Berline's world became smaller and smaller. She couldn't leave the house unless someone led her by the hand; couldn't even go outside for fresh air unless someone took her. Most days were spent in bed enduring pain, except for twice-weekly dialysis trips or visits for laser treatments. We spoke by phone as frequently as we could, but even being on the phone when she felt so sick wasn't something she could manage often.

My sister Ruth began spending time with Berline during the day, taking care of her while Don was at work. It became clear to me as I wrote this story that in caring for the dying in North

Carolina, Ruth took on their pain and holds it in her body now. I don't think she was ever able to get past this pain—unable to allow herself to get well because she wouldn't have thought she should be well when her mother and sisters had died. Those are my thoughts, and I could be wrong, but that's what I saw in her. Maybe she has shed the pain, but I don't think so.

Ruth stayed with Berline many hours to keep her company and help her through the long, painful days. The thought comes to me that it should have been me. I wonder if I should have moved back home, even though moving back would have been a living death for me because I couldn't bear to be in the place that held so many painful memories. Yet maybe I should have moved back anyway.

Don would say, "You know, just about the time you'd call, Berline would be saying she thought she should call you. It was like you both knew when each was thinking of the other and knew you needed to talk. It would usually happen that one of us would call the other, just to check in. There was a connection, a knowing—we were apart, yet together.

Berline's pain was like a jagged dagger slashing my insides. No matter what I was doing, the ripping and tearing coursed through me. Sometimes it was almost more than I could bear. I walked almost every day, praying to God to heal her body and give her release from pain. Some days I raged at Him, other times I begged. For months on end, I prayed for Berline, but she didn't get better.

Yet again, I wondered if there was a God. Finally, I just prayed for Him to do His will—to do whatever He wanted. I released her to Him. I felt inside that releasing her to God was what I needed to do, but it took me a long time to get there. I'd wanted to do something to save her, but finally it became clear that to save her, I had to release her.

On August 14, 1991, around noon, Berline called me. She didn't call often anymore, so I knew something was more wrong than usual. She was very weak, and I strained to hear her.

"The doctors say I need another heart surgery," her labored voice informed me, "and I don't think I can do it."

She started crying as she continued. "If I thought it would really make me better, then I guess I would do it, but I'm tired and I just don't think I can go through another surgery."

I choked back my own tears. "Berline, you need to make the decision that's right for you. I love you and support you in whatever decision you make. It's okay. You don't need to go through another surgery. It's okay to make that decision."

As we talked, it was clear she needed me to understand why she couldn't go through another surgery. She needed my understanding so I would let her go. I didn't realize at the time it would be the last time we'd ever talk.

As we said goodbye that day, I told Berline I was going camping for a couple of days with Cliff. He and I had planned to go to Alta Lake in Eastern Washington. He'd already gone ahead, and I was to follow the next day. My daughters were with their dad for the weekend—a rare occurrence—so it was a good opportunity for Cliff and I to get away and relax.

I arrived at the campground late that afternoon where, true to his nature, Cliff had set up the tent and cooked dinner for us. The weather was warm with a slight breeze that kept it from being too hot, and the smell of fir trees and campfires scented the air.

After dinner we sat beside the campfire, relaxing and enjoying the outdoors and our time away from life's chores. Cliff is always so good about cooking when we camp—great vegetables, usually hamburgers or hot dogs, then roasting marshmallows over the open fire. He's been the first person in my life most concerned about me and what I want, ready to do whatever makes me happy. I was feeling very fortunate to have him that night as the pain of talking to Berline and her suffering loomed over me.

Despite the fun we were having, a shadow like a blue hue hung over and around me. I tried to push it aside and concentrate on having a relaxing time with Cliff. I'd become very good at pushing things aside, but no matter what I did that night, the pain and fear stayed with me. I kept silent about it, however, determined to allow us to enjoy our surroundings and time together.

Usually when tent camping with only a lantern for illumination, we turned in shortly after darkness fell—in August, after 9 p.m. After dinner and roasting marshmallows, we climbed into our tent and lay down on sleeping bags we'd placed on an air mattress. This made a comfortable bed, and because I was physically tired from the trip and emotionally tired from pain, I expected to sleep like a lamb that night. But that was not to be.

As soon as I lay down, all the pent-up emotions came erupting over me like a heavy dark cloud ready to drop its first sprinkles of rain. But there would be no relief tonight as the heavy cloud continued forming larger. I turned one way, then another, trying to still my mind with deep breathing exercises, but had no success. Sometime after 2 a.m., my body exhausted, I dropped off to sleep only to begin dreaming in vivid detail. But my dream was really a nightmare with Berline as the main character.

In my dream, I'd called home and was talking to somebody, though I couldn't tell who.

"Berline has gone," they said.

"What do you mean, gone?" I practically screamed.

"She died last night," they answered.

"No! No! No! No!" I was screaming, and I couldn't seem to stop. Then I hung up the phone.

The whole scenario played out in slow, excruciating detail in my dream, and when I woke up, I was still screaming, "No!"

Cliff heard me and rolled over. "What's wrong?"

"I dreamed Berline died," I answered as he put his arms around me to comfort me.

"Well, that wouldn't surprise you really, would it?" His reply was as much a statement as a question.

"Of course it would!" I snapped at him.

How could he say that? Of course, I didn't really think she was going to die—she couldn't really die! Without going into more detail about the dream, I got up and got dressed.

Cliff followed and made coffee and breakfast for us. The eggs and bacon cooked in the warm morning air seemed to be just what I needed to get going and feel a little better. I was afraid to say more, even though I didn't really believe the old wives' tale that telling someone your dreams before breakfast made them come true. Anyway, I said no more about my dream as we ate breakfast.

While we were having our after-breakfast cup of coffee, the overpowering urge to call home struck me, pushing me to call immediately. In 1991, cell phones weren't nearly as prevalent as today, so neither of us had one. Luckily there was a phone booth at the campground entrance, so I took my calling card and walked over to call home. I dialed Berline's house—no answer. I called my sister Ruth.

Before I could explain my call, Ruth exclaimed, "I'm so glad you called. I didn't know how to get in touch with you."

"Why?" I asked, as fear mounted in my chest.

She told me exactly what happened, just as my dream had depicted. Even the words were the same. I found myself screaming, "No!" and hanging up the phone. My dream had foretold exactly what had happened. Did Berline come to me in my dream to tell me goodbye? Did she come so I would call and find out she had died? I do not know.

I ran back to our campsite, crying and screaming, tears streaming down my face. Cliff ran out to meet me, and I buried my face in his shoulder, crying until I thought my insides would seep out through my tears. We broke camp and began our four-hour drive home so I could go to my twin sister's funeral.

Dear God, I truly hadn't thought she would die. No matter how much you think you're ready, can you ever be ready? I was not.

So many things were wrong with Berline's body that it's hard to say what the actual cause of death was. No matter—she was gone. I believe she had called me to ask me to let her go, to make sure I knew she couldn't fight the battle any longer. It was the same night she'd been taken to the hospital. She told Don she didn't want to be put on a machine and didn't want to be brought back. She wanted to be let go!

Berline had been such a fighter, working long and hard to get better but only getting worse—she'd been fighting for several years. Maybe if she'd only been blind, she could have dealt with that, would have learned to get around and not only survive but thrive. But there were too many things wrong with her. Her body was rebelling, and there was nothing she could do.

I thought of her words when Mama died: "Did she just stop breathing like a little bird?" I couldn't help but wonder if that was how Berline died. Did she just stop breathing like a tiny bird with that last little wispy breath?

With the family around her at the hospital, Berline let go, and in my dream I knew she was gone. The pain of losing her was the most terrible thing I'd ever felt—like part of my life had been wrenched out of me. Like part of me was gone, maybe the best part. Through the years, I'd come to think of her as the best part of us. Half of me was now missing, and I would never be the same, would never be whole again.

I cried all the way home—four long hours of tears, but there would be many more. My eyes were swollen and red, crying and driving, remembering and hurting. *Oh my God, she was gone. I had given her up to You and You took her. Why couldn't it be that You saved her? What was the reason she had to go?*

Grief

Tears streaming down my face, dripping off my chin—Who cares? My twin sister is dead.

Why do these people act as if nothing is happening when my twin is dead?

My chest hurts, begs for release; there is no release. As many as I let drop, many more come—they don't want to stop.

My breath hurts, my chest hurts, the pit in my stomach feels like a boulder—a heavy jagged rock ripping and tearing up through my body, breaking into a thousand tiny pieces, flushing out my nose and eyes.

I think my chest will burst; I must be going mad with this pain that I'm in.

Oh my God, my twin is dead.

We drove home to Seattle, then I flew to North Carolina, arriving in time for the traditional lying-in wait the next night.

As I walked into the funeral home for the services, Don came over to me.

"We tried to call you," he said. "We didn't know how to get in touch with you, and we were afraid you wouldn't get here in time for Berline's funeral." He seemed relieved and satisfied somehow as he continued, **"I knew Berline would call you, and she did."**

Don was like the host at a dinner party, making sure everyone was taken care of. It never ceases to amaze me that even though our loved one is lying there dead, the politeness and niceties continue as if it's a normal day.

Berline's body rested in her coffin at the front of the room, but I don't know what it looked like because I refused to look at it. I couldn't bear to see her body inside that cold box, no matter how elegant it might be. As family and friends milled about and went up to view her body, my own body convulsed with waves of revulsion. Wherever Berline's soul may be, it certainly wasn't in that now-cold body lying in a coffin.

I made myself promises that I would never lie in wait, never have my body lying in a coffin for my family and friends to view. Even as I was thinking this, I knew Berline was accustomed to this Southern tradition and would have expected and accepted this day as it played out. So my twin sister's body lay there while people milled around and talked.

Don brought out his camera and snapped pictures of her in her coffin, then had each of their sons stand by her body while he took their pictures. Following them, he had the grandchildren gather around, and he took pictures of them all together as well. I thought it would never end as he continued taking pictures. I watched in horror. It was like a trip to the beach, and they were all having their snapshots taken.

My chest started to constrict. I felt like I was suffocating. It took all my strength to keep from doubling over in pain. I had to get outside for a while—inside it felt like I was running, but outside I kept up the Southern tradition of hiding hurt, watching manners.

Don walked over to me and politely asked, "Do you want to have your picture taken with Berline?"

My face must have shown my shock.

"No, I don't," I managed to rasp.

"Does my taking these pictures bother you?" he asked.

"No, it's okay," I lied, and before any more could be said, I strode out into the night air.

My brother James followed me, and we almost fell into each other's arms as the pain overtook us. We held each other and cried until the tears gave us a short reprieve. Through our tears, we laughed together about how long it took Berline to say something, about her temper and how she used to chase him up a tree with a butcher knife. We cried and we laughed, and we each died a little inside. Then we went back into the viewing to do our Southern duties.

Southern Duties

Now in the South we smile politely and shake your hand. We've been taught to be charming even though the time is alarming.

No matter my sister, my twin, my half is dead, I have my duties as a Southern girl born and bred.

Wipe the tears away, hide them inside smile and talk of things that no one cares about when my other half lays there dead.

Yes, I live out West, four daughters and divorced. No, I won't be moving back to the South.

Oh yes, what a shame My family endures so much pain. Our family is dying, My twin sister is dead.

And oh by the way where in the hell were you when we were kids with no food and no one to care, with handouts at the church door?

Thank you for coming. Yes, she is so beautiful. They did an excellent job hiding the creases of suffering, covering the shadows of pain her face has known.

No, we were different, her and I, and no, I do not yet have the disease that kills and maims and brings so much pain.

Yes, how lucky I am, and thank you so much for reminding me.

All this Southern style and foolery I'm a Southern girl, I am.

Berline's funeral was the next day. Don asked me to ride with him in the family car and sit beside him at her services, which I did. He needed me and me him; I guess. It was a bright, sunny, warm day, and she had beautiful flowers, but she was gone.

We had a memorial service at the church first where our nephew's wife sang the song Berline had chosen. Don said she was always asking, "Why me, Lord? Why this pain? Why can't I get well? Why do I have this disease?" So, it was fitting she chose "Why Me, Lord" for her funeral service.

Why me, Lord?

What have I ever done to deserve even one

of the pleasures I've known.

Why? Why indeed, I question. Why her, why us, why our family? Were we just born to suffer and die, or is there more?

After the memorial service at the church, we were driven out to the gravesite. I rode with Don and their little granddaughter in the family car. We rode in silence, holding each other's hands in that big black limousine on the way to bury Berline. She was buried beside Mama. Seems they'd decided to buy those plots together, like they knew they'd soon need them.

Don and I and her granddaughter sat in the front row of chairs and listened and watched as they lowered her into the ground. The pain washes over me like a wet blanket, too heavy to move, so it just lies on top and begins to smother me. My body feels the dampness from the blanket, and though the sun is warm, my body is wet, cold, and heavy with pain.

The crushing weight on me, in me feels like I will burst open and I will suffocate. My throat is tight, my head aches, and my stomach feels like a newly gutted animal must feel, with his wound ripped open. I cannot breathe. I must stuff this inside for a while. Maybe, just maybe, one day I'll be able to take these feelings out, look at them, and let them go. But not today. Not today.

Once the services were over, we did the traditional thing—went back to my brother's house to sit around, eat, and talk. We talked of things that had no meaning and some that did. My older brother, who had always been the hell-raiser, the one who lost his temper and ruled with an iron hand, seemed like a beaten man. He had the disease now and heart problems too. He was on medication. His face was gray and weary—no longer the hell-raiser of his youth but a worn-out man, grateful to his wife for being there and loving him.

When it was time to end the day, since there were so many of us, James and Roma stayed with my brother, and I went to stay at Berline's home with Don. We talked for a while of Berline and who she had been and what she'd been forced to endure over the last several years.

Don brought out Berline's jewelry and told me I could take a few items. As I looked through her jewelry, all the memories of her wearing them flooded over me, and I found myself loath to touch them, to take away her touch, her smell, the essence of her. Knowing I was leaving in the morning, I pushed the feelings aside and looked at each piece.

To my surprise, I found a bracelet with a green, emerald setting that wasn't unusual, except that it matched exactly a ring I'd purchased some years earlier! Without either of us talking about it, we'd purchased jewelry with the exact same stone and setting. Don told me Berline always knew things about me and was very connected to me, even though we lived more than three thousand miles apart. He told me she knew when to call me and likewise, when I would call her.

Before she'd gotten sick, Berline had wanted a short fur jacket, which Don bought for her. She'd never worn the jacket because she'd gotten so sick, so it was in storage. Don told me about it and the next day took it out and gave it to me. I have the jacket, but I've never worn it. Each time I look at it, I see Berline's face and wish she'd been able to be here long enough to wear it.

I took a few other pieces of jewelry that night, and I cherish each one now—something of her but not like I needed any material thing to remember her by. Just to have them because she touched them, wore them, and loved them. Years before, Mama had given Berline and me matching porcelain dolls, and I really wanted to ask Don for this doll, but he didn't offer, and I didn't ask. But maybe one day I will.

The evening ended, so we prepared to go to bed. Don slept in the same place he had for years, only this time Berline's side of the bed remained empty and cold. I slept on the sofa in their living room, but it seemed the night didn't want to be quiet.

I tossed and turned and finally slept, or at least I slept just enough to dream. I was awake and asleep—the type of sleep that just sits at the top of your brain but doesn't really give you any rest or reprieve. After a while I was just awake with the feeling that somebody was in the room, somebody or something that was evil.

The air was alive with it, so heavy and real it was as if I could reach out and touch this thing. I tried to shrink myself down into the covers to hide. I told myself I was crazy—this was not real. But the fact that I couldn't see it didn't matter. My whole body felt its presence, so alive and so strong it nearly suffocated me.

It was a feeling, a thought, a wicked presence that washed over me and wanted to consume me. The thoughts, like words spoken aloud, popped into my head: "Your sister is dead. I came for her. I wanted her, but she escaped, so I will take you instead."

Death Not Satisfied

I feel death, I smell death, I taste death, I am death— I can't escape death.

Death says, *I've come for you—your sister I didn't get.*

Death calls, *I'll take you instead.*

No, I cried, or did I whimper? No, Death, you can't have me. She beat you and set the prelude for me to win as well.

She took up the battle cry. She was stronger than you. She escaped you.

These words were just as real as if a person was standing there saying these things to me. I sat upright, still trying to make believe it wasn't true, that it was all in my head. Did I really believe in evil spirits? Was I somehow imagining this or dreaming this? What was wrong with me? There had been so much hurt and emotion these last few days, I told myself, so my imagination is running away with me.

But I knew this was real. There had been other times in my life when my body had known and felt evil around me—evil that threatened to consume me, and thoughts that popped into my head unbidden. This part of me that knows and sees things that are not of this physical world, not unlike an old friend, comes to visit so that you recognize and know them without many words —this feeling, this knowing. This was real!

Terrified that I couldn't escape, and feeling as if it were smothering me, I finally couldn't endure it any longer. I jumped up and ran into the bedroom with Don. Don didn't seem too surprised when I told him I was having nightmares and wanted to stay with him. He moved over to give me Berline's spot in their bed.

I lay there beside him, in her spot, the place where Berline had lain all those years. The equipment that had kept her alive for the last couple of years was still there beside the bed, and I thought: *How strange to lie in the bed beside my twin sister's husband, her dead and buried that day.* But I was too terrified to go back into the other room, so there I stayed with Don's arm draped over me until morning.

Now my rational mind tells me I was imagining things, but my other mind knows I was not. For me to sleep in her bed, in her place, beside her husband—I know the terror was there; otherwise, this is not something I would ever have done. Whatever that evil was, I'm glad to know it didn't get Berline, that she fought the fight and didn't give in, didn't let this thing take her and win.

Berline's Spiritual Battle

She fought the battle between earth and fire, God and hell.

In pain and dying, she did not give in to the evil that lay in wait to claim her soul.

Struggle she might, question for sure, but never did she turn from Your door.

Even in the end, to You she called to take her home, leaving the devil, the evil one waiting, wishing for a soul to devour.

But my sister woke me and said, get up and get out. Do not let this ghoul get you instead!

Go to my husband, my protector, my friend, and he will guard you this one night.

I flew home the next day to my daughters, my job, and school, determined to live my life as if I had only one day to live. After all, what else did we have? I bought another ring, thinking to fill this emptiness inside.

Blue Sapphire Ring Poem

I bought a ring, a blue Sapphire to cover the hurt and hide my fear.

Blue as the ocean deep, sharp as the mountain steep, icy glacier melting weeps, waves roll out their sleep.

Gave me a place to hide just long enough to carry me through the tide—a little space inside before my pain bashes me on the rocks of the ocean floor.

I questioned God as I'd done in the past and wondered if He truly was real, and if so, then how could He let this happen and why? Death seemed to be as much a part of me as life, so I sped things up. I didn't think there was much time to be had, so I continued at a pace that many would have thought crazy. I worked my job during the day, went to school two nights a week and on weekends.

Somehow going up that corporate ladder, and getting there fast, felt like the thing to do. After all, wouldn't money and prestige bring peace and happiness? Occasionally I allowed myself to feel the pain, so I thought I was dealing with it, but maybe it's never truly dealt with. I don't know, don't have the answers, but my life was so fast there wasn't much time to think or feel. Maybe that's what I wanted.

Many nights I drove home from school without even knowing where I was on the road. I would seem to just start, suddenly awake, then try to figure out where I was and if I'd missed my exit to home. I'm quite sure my three daughters at home suffered a great deal from this—from my fast pace, my not being home, and of course having a father who only cared about how he could hurt me. But those hidden feelings drove me onward, regardless of the havoc left in their path.

Life traveled on as it does, with or without you totally conscious of it, or of who you are, with your one life to live. I was very fortunate to have Cliff in my life along this path—he was kind and sensitive, and when he held me, I felt protected and warm. I can't ever remember feeling warm before him. I wanted to stay in his arms and let him hold me and make all the rest of the world go away.

We had many ups and downs in our relationship, but all that is another story. Suffice it to say for now he was here, and I needed him. But true to form, I kept a barrier up and made sure he knew I was going to make my own decisions and that I would never be dependent on a mere man again. I loved him for his gentleness, for his love for me, and for just being able to talk with him as another adult—something I had not had with my former husband.

When I think of the protective shell around me, I think of an eggshell—hard, with some cracks in it, but easy enough to crack open at the right time. But it was time that I needed. I had to make my way in the world; to be sure I was a whole person, that I could take care of myself and would never allow another man to treat me the way my ex-husband had. Our lives moved along their path as the changing seasons of the year—one day warm and sunny, the next rainy and cold, but continually moving and changing.

When Berline died, half of me died with her. There was a new hole inside me, a gaping open wound. Then there was the guilt —the guilt of being the healthy twin, the one left behind. Why was it that she had all the sickness and agony and I was healthy? And where was God in all this?

Unbearable guilt at taking all the good genes and letting my sister die consumed me. If I had gotten just half of what she carried, then she might be alive. We could each have shared the body harm, but we would both be here. I wondered why God didn't do that. Where is He anyway? What decisions for us does He make? Are we truly children of God, a God who cares one way or another how we feel, of the pain we are in? I was no longer sure God was there or that He indeed even existed.

Eternal Twins

Twins we were, twins we are, and twins we stay—no matter she died and went away.

She left me here to face each day, a pair ripped asunder, two lives torn apart, two mirror-image crystals—we shared a common bond.

Twins indeed, me and you, me to stay, you to go.

Lilacs in the field, blue daffodils, ocean blue—so am I.

You left me here to cry for you!

Somewhere inside I decided this was all there was to life, so I better grab what I wanted and get what I dared. That was my motto for the next several years.

CHAPTER 9
THE SPECIAL SISTER

I had been juggling school during Mama and Berline's illnesses and deaths, and now I was building a career. True to our family's entrepreneurial spirit, I'd struck out on my own with a training and consulting business. After a couple of years, I joined Oracle as a consultant, implementing business software and training end users. The work required constant travel, but I'd finished my master's degree and was focused on building my career.

While navigating a difficult period with my partner, Cliff, and juggling three teenage daughters, I chose to examine what I truly wanted, finding profound guidance in a book called "Divorce Busting" that helped transform our relationship. This was my life when the next two deaths struck our family.

My oldest sister Bertha was next to die. She'd been sick for years —lupus, chronic pain, one ailment after another. Despite her constant illness, I never imagined she was sick enough to die.

One family story about Bertha gave us endless occasions to laugh. Part of one of Bertha's fingers was missing, and the tale of how it happened became family legend. On our farm, Daddy kept a chopping block in the yard for cutting wood. The story goes that Roman, Gaston, and Bertha—the eldest children— were cutting wood when an argument erupted. Supposedly, Bertha laid her hand on the chopping block and dared Gaston to cut off a finger. Gaston of course denied that, but the story lived on.

However it really happened, he cut off part of a finger. I still remember that stub—her badge of courage through the years. You knew better than to mess with Bertha too much.

Other happy memories I have of Bertha cemented our lifelong love for each other. When I was fifteen, my then-husband and I moved to Virginia where he was stationed at the Army base near Newport News. She was only seven years older than me, and it was during this time that **Bertha and I became friends rather than just sisters.** We were inseparable. We ran errands, went shopping, ate at Hardee's and spent lots of time together during the week, and on weekends, we played cards with our husbands. We must have lived there for well over a year, and those get-togethers made it an incredibly fun and happy time. Bertha and my husband would tease each other and play slap, creating memories we all laughed about for years.

Looking back now, it is eye-opening to realize how very young we both were—I was a 15-year-old teenager, and she was barely in her early twenties with a house full of children. We felt so old then, but now, with fifteen and twenty-one-year-old granddaughters, I have a totally different perspective on how much responsibility she carried as a young girl.

A Young Bertha

Bertha married young and had six kids. A husband who drank too much.

her life filled up, spilled over with pain.

Too many kids for such a young girl, Too much hurt for one to endure.

Without skills to cope, she buried the pain inside.

Food became her escape from a life lived spiraling out of control, though no one ever saw her eat more than a bite.

and the more pain, the more she grew, and there was no pill to pull her out of the hole life dug.

Bertha married young and was overwhelmed by responsibility before most women would be ready. She had two children by the time she was nineteen, two more by twenty-one, and the next two by the time she was twenty-six. To have six children before her mid-twenties—when many young women are still in school—must have been devastatingly overwhelming for a shy young girl with no worldly experience. She gained weight with her first pregnancy, and because the children came so fast, each successive birth added more pounds that never left her. I only recently realized how shy and quiet she was and that she must have hidden inside any sadness she had in life.

While her husband was very attentive in later years, he drank heavily early on and hurt her emotionally many times. They were always struggling financially, and it must have been over-whelming at times.

My happiest memories of her were watching her in the kitchen cooking and what a cook she was. There was nothing she couldn't make, whether a meal or a dessert. She was a wonderful cook, and she loved cooking and visiting and laughing with us as she cooked. Either making meals or baking desserts, her food was the best. I think she was the best cook I ever knew. No matter what she cooked, it was wonderful. I know her and her husband considered opening a cafe but were just never able to swing it. But her cooking was notoriously amazing. She would manage to use every pot and pan in the kitchen when she cooked however so there were always lots of dishes to wash after a meal. Mama's homemade biscuits were wonderful, but I must admit that Bertha's were a little bit better. Not that we ever told Mama that of course.

A funny story that was a family talk about around the kitchen table story, that would be told and retold many times, included her numerous dishes she would use while cooking. When she was pregnant with one of her children, she had cooked a big meal and had dishes all over the kitchen and dining room. She went into labor right after the meal and before cleaning up and had to go into the hospital to have the baby. Joe her husband stacked up all the dishes in the oven and the refrigerator and anywhere else he could put them so the kitchen would look clean when she came home from the hospital. However, they were dirty dishes and not clean dishes that were hidden everywhere. I can't even imagine what her face looked like when she saw the dishes stacked in the oven and refrigerator. She had a good sense of humor so I'm sure she must have laughed about it but then most likely yelled at him to wash them. We all laughed about that episode for years.

Bertha always made us, her sisters and brothers feel like we were the most important people in the world to her. She made each of us feel special and that we were her special sister or brother. After her death my brother and I talked about it and found out that each of us had lived our lives believing that we were her special sister or brother and that she loved us the best. It was such a wonderful thing for her to do as we didn't get that feeling from anyone else in our lives.

I always remember her in bed for long stretches of the day. As her body grew larger, getting up and moving around became more difficult, creating a vicious cycle of decreased activity and increased weight. While she tried many times to lose weight, she was in a constant, frustrating battle to get proper medical care. She visited doctor after doctor trying to find a diagnosis and help for her worsening health issues. As she described it, they all focused solely on her weight: they blamed all her issues on being overweight and refused to look any further. While excess weight certainly aggravated her health problems, it was clear that she suffered from unaddressed illnesses. Her struggle became a demoralizing loop: feeling desperately unwell and seeking help, only to be dismissed with the prescription that losing weight would solve all her problems. This lack of comprehensive care left her with unidentified and untreated root causes, making her situation feel insurmountable.

When Bertha had her seventh child, a daughter, she and her husband were older with fewer children at home. She seemed less overwhelmed, so this daughter received the benefits of parents being more ready for a baby.

Since I lived in the Northwest during Bertha's final years, I'm unclear on all her health details. To me, she was constantly sick, and never able to get any help that made a difference. She often spoke of her pain, though it didn't seem to be the family curse of diabetes. She'd been diagnosed with lupus, but I'm not sure what else.

I remember Bertha telling me her husband had to help her use the bathroom, get dressed, and care for her in the most intimate ways. The years in the beginning of their marriage he was wild and always seemed to be in trouble and hurting her but in the later years she told me how much he helped her and how much she loved him because he did all those things for her.

Along with the physical pain and suffering of illness, the loss of independence and pride must be horrendous to accept. Like Berline, Bertha became dependent on her husband as a loving caregiver in her final years, assisting her with the most basic and intimate needs.

I often think about how we spend our lives trying to maintain dignity and independence, only to age and lose the ability to handle our most private needs. We enter the world as babies needing diaper changes and someone to wipe our mouths and bottoms. In severe illness and aging, we return to being helpless, needing assistance with basic needs. We leave as we arrive.

How sad that we often don't receive the same love and tenderness in death that we receive in birth.

In 1995, Bertha was admitted to the hospital. Since she was sick often, none of us siblings were immediately alarmed. Our perception was that this was just another prolonged illness; we understood she was dealing with an infection that wouldn't heal, but we believed it was only a matter of time before she recovered and came home. I was told the doctors repeatedly assured the family that she would be fine, even going so far as to tell her husband and children they were "catering to her too much" and should leave her alone.

This shared belief that the illness was not serious made the fast turn of events even more devastating. While she was hospitalized, I called her, but we spoke only briefly—she was in too much pain to continue, and listening to her misery brought back that familiar sensation of a knife tearing through my insides. I found myself avoiding calling back.

She'd said, "Call me back," and I'd agreed, but almost a week passed without contact. A week isn't long when you're busy working, raising daughters, and mending a broken relationship. But a week in the hospital, waiting for someone to call and show they care that you're hurting, lonely, and questioning whether you'll live or die—then a week is an eternity.

She called one morning, saying she wasn't sure I knew she could talk. Instead of telling her the truth—that I loved her so much her pain became mine and I couldn't tolerate more—I covered my real feelings. I said, "Oh, you know, I've just been too busy."

I wanted to take those words back immediately. When I said, "just too busy," I heard her sharp intake of breath and knew I'd wounded her. That was the last time I spoke with my sister when she could respond.

The next family contact came suddenly when my niece called: "You better come fast." Despite the previous assurances from the doctors, Bertha had rapidly declined and could no longer speak —she just stared at her children and husband, already letting go. The change was so sudden that the doctors had to change their advice and tell the family to return immediately. I tried talking to her by phone, pleading with her not to give up, not to let go, but the distance was too great. She died before I could get there. Bertha was only 52 years old when she died.

Too Late

Too late, I was too late to say the things I should have said,

to hold your hand and rub your feet, to gently caress your brow and whisper as sisters will:

It's okay to let go, to feel no more the aches your body brings. Liberate yourself from days and nights filled with cascading pain—the torrential pour that rips and chips, eats away at who you are and who you were.

Pain that lives within made your life a living hell, caused you to retreat inside to hide, again and again inside your mind— retreating to block life from getting in.

Pain of your body, aching pain, searing, grabbing, hot piercing pain begs you to stay.

My heart says go—get out of this life that brought you so much pain.

There must be a place of rest and relief, a place to retreat.

If all is lost, at least it won't be like this.

Life is full of "should haves," but "should haves" are too late. She was gone.

I attended her funeral. She lay in her casket, and once again we had the viewing night. I saw Don, Berline's husband, who had met someone and married quickly. He asked if I felt Berline, if she came to me. I said yes, sometimes so real it was as if she stood right beside me. He said sometimes he saw her at the foot of his bed. She was still there, part of him, still talking to him.

I wanted to run away again from this South, this place where it seemed my family endured so much pain. I considered the life Bertha had lived, how hard it appeared to be. But even so she lived and loved and enjoyed her children and was there as much as she could be for them. She seemed to hold her pain within.

I think I've been running all my life to find better, to do better, to gain one more piece of knowledge that will make me better, so I won't ever have to live again as I did in childhood.

We held her funeral, then I stayed at Roman's that night, talking about Bertha and life. Gaston was there—he was so rarely present during my visits, and it felt good to see and talk with him. It was bittersweet, discussing old times while our sisters died around us.

I told both brothers that night I wouldn't return home for another funeral. I'd visit them while they were alive, but I'd never travel south again for a funeral. They said they understood—I hope they did, because when the time came to make that decision, I kept my word and didn't return for the next two funerals.

As I write today, I feel the familiar strain of sadness, knowing that regardless of knowledge or where I run, I take myself wherever I go. This sadness is not a passing mood; it is a permanent echo of the pain this life has held—a pain my body is reluctant to release.

My commitment now is not to conquer this sadness, but to continuously battle the heavy "body memories" so they do not win the war. I must remain vigilant, aware of the risk that, like my sisters, I could die before my time. The vulnerability of aging and losing strength is real, but so is the will to keep fighting.

I may not know how to prevent the sadness from residing within me, but I know how to handle the day I'm in. I know I can choose honesty over concealment, presence over avoidance, and love over the hurt. That is the lesson Bertha's death left me with —a difficult, vital compass I must continue to follow.

CHAPTER 10
THE CONTAGIOUS LAUGH

Carol was in the hospital undergoing dialysis when Bertha died, fighting to rid her heart and lungs of deadly fluid buildup. She'd lost most kidney function and was sick constantly—her body unable to eliminate the poisons slowly killing her from within.

She'd developed Type 1 diabetes in her early twenties, giving herself injections for as long as I can remember. In her early forties, heart disease joined the assault, requiring open-heart surgery.

I've always wondered about the name "sugar diabetes"—only recently shortened to just "diabetes." Sugar brings to mind sweetness: melt-in-your-mouth chocolate, delicious pies, fluffy coconut cakes. But this sugar isn't sweet, pleasant, or good. It's vicious and evil, robbing you of health, independence, and finally life itself—or the lives of those you love. It viciously attacks, robs, maims, and kills.

Carol had crossed eyes, so you never knew who she was looking at or talking to. I'm sure she got tired of constantly having to clarify, "I'm talking to you." Today her eyes would have been fixed, but with no money and without the knowledge of medical treatments, it wasn't even possible. When you are poor you never think about or even know of things that might help you. There is no way to afford those things anyway as they are out of your realm of possibilities.

She had beautiful thick red hair, stood about 5'4", and was tiny most of her life. Freckles dotted her face, and she had full lips—the kind people pay for today. She was beautiful, but in her eyes and heart, she could never quite believe it herself. I remember during visits home we would head to the store and spend most of the time sitting in the car talking. It was nice to have those alone times to catch up and find out what things were happening in each other's lives. It seemed there were always things she wanted to change in her life but never knew how to. Not unlike most of us it's easy to know there are things we don't like but much harder to know how to fix them.

Those were good times no matter what we talked about. Time to be alone and get to know each other better as adults. She had a special quality of being able to laugh at herself no matter how serious the conversation might be. She loved people and life even though life dealt her a very hard path with her sickness. We could sit talking and laughing for hours on end and then hurry into the store to get whatever we had gone for. I've seen in my lifetime that most girls and women just need to talk. They need to talk things out with someone else, and many times are not looking for advice but just the simple act of talking about things in our lives helps us to solve issues and feel better about things in general. I loved that we had each other for that when I would visit.

Later in her life she started doing many creative artistic things. She had talent, she had courage, she had strength, she had kindness, she had love, she had devotion. She never appeared to be able to believe herself special, but our family knew she was and appreciated her. Carol was Mamas right arm so to speak. Always there for Mama when many of us were away or doing other things. I know that Mama depended on her.

Carol's laugh was contagious—it seemed to start at her feet and work its way up. Her laugh lives inside me still; it was spontaneous and wonderful. When it reached her mouth, she'd clap her hand over it, not wanting anyone to see it wide open with joy. She was amazing and we all knew it. I don't think she and I ever had a cross word with each other which is amazing as sisters will usually have some arguments growing up.

As I write about each sister, I think, "Now she's my favorite," only to feel the same about the next. I found them all extraordinary, and Carol was no exception. She worked incredibly hard, sometimes holding two jobs while raising her daughters, unselfishly giving to her husband and children. After exhausting workdays, she would go home to take care of her family. She was such a worker I'm not sure she would have been happy not working outside the home, but I personally cannot imagine the strength and courage it took to have Type 1 diabetes and still go out to work every day.

She met her husband while he was in the army—he was very handsome with dark hair and exotic complexion. She thought herself incredibly lucky to find someone so good-looking who loved her. Life showed he was also the lucky one, they didn't always get along but they loved each other through it and spent many years together.

After the army, her husband went into sales as a career. He did various types of sales and sometimes the money was good and sometimes times were hard. He was a good salesperson and appeared to enjoy the work. Carol had a variety of jobs, but I don't really remember her never not working until later in her life. Now that I understand what diabetes would have done to her, I'm even more impressed that she was able to work and keep up the way she did.

They moved away from North Carolina briefly, but Carol and Mama were so close that being separated was torture. They returned and never lived more than a few miles from Mama again. I always remember Carol stopping by for lunch or coffee during work breaks. She'd eat with Mama, then rush home to take care of her family. I often wondered if Mama timed these visits to ensure Carol got enough to eat since she was so small. As a mother one is likely to attempt to make sure your child, no matter the age, eats enough.

They lived in the same neighborhood as we did at one time, and they would buy chocolate milk from the delivery milkman. While they went off to work some of us kids would sneak over and drink some of their chocolate milk. It is funny to me now and my goodness that was the best chocolate milk I ever had but

I'm sure it drove them a little nuts for us kids to be taking their stuff while they were out working. During one period after both families had moved and we were a few miles apart, I went to live with them for some reason. I'm not sure why or how long it was or how old I was. All I remember is doing it and them taking me out and buying me clothes. For someone who always had hand me downs that was an amazing experience and I can remember being so happy with my clothes. I honestly don't remember Mama ever being able to take us out and buy us clothes, so this was a very special event for me and a lifelong memory. Her husband was also the one who saved me from a couple of bad experiences with men much older than I so I'm eternally grateful to him for that.

The image of Carol and Mama giving themselves injections is forever etched in my memory. When Carol stopped for break-fast, they'd prepare their shots, pull up their blouses, roll down their pants, and inject themselves—pinching flesh to slide the needles in. I'd sit watching this with a feeling of horror and they of course had over the course of time gotten used to it as it was a daily routine.

In later years, she showed her creativity through making beau-tiful flower arrangements. She possessed abundant talent and abilities never used to full potential as her health was a huge limiting factor.

I wonder if people with fathers—especially fathers who love and support you—know how lucky they were. What a difference having a daddy could have made in our lives; one who made us feel special could have saved us all so much pain and heartache.

It could have saved our children from pain and heartache passed down from generation to generation.

Even when we don't want to, we repeat childhood patterns with our children—patterns that continue for generations, requiring education and determination to change what was set in motion years before. But that takes a lot of work and self-knowledge and some of that self-knowledge we don't gain until we are older.

Carol was always frail yet took on so much. She was shaky with frequent blackouts throughout her diabetic years. Hospital visits became routine as her body spiraled downward. She might win battles, but the war was never over—never to be won.

During and after heart surgery, she withered to skin and bones, never the same physically or emotionally. Watching my siblings' experiences made me wary of surgery, though one never knows what they'll do when the time comes.

She bore a huge chest scar from surgery, taking two to three years to feel even a little bit okay. Living 3,000 miles away, seeing her only during infrequent visits, I was shocked by how she'd aged and changed after surgery.

She spent recovery time with Mama because she couldn't rest at home. She needed care, and to be somewhere other than home as the things to do at home are always waiting for you so you never quite rest when one should. After heart surgery, she declared she wouldn't do anything to prolong life again. When the time came, she'd just let it happen.

When the time did come, pain and suffering were so severe she couldn't just let it happen. Her kidneys failed, lungs filled with fluid. She stayed home as long as possible, but when pain became unbearable, she checked into the hospital for help.

Carol was hospitalized when Bertha died. We all expected Carol to go first, but Bertha preceded her, and no one wanted to break the news to her. There is so much pain in watching sisters die.

I attended Bertha's funeral and visited Carol in the hospital, having no idea how to comfort her. She and Bertha had grown very close in recent years, so Bertha's death devastated her. Carol cried, repeating, "She went before me; I thought I'd go first, but she went before me."

Carol and I discussed Bertha's death and Berline's struggle—all those surgeries Berline endured trying to stay alive. Carol told me she hadn't wanted hospitalization, had decided against another heart surgery or heroic life-saving measures.

Carol looked so sad when she said, "I just didn't know it would be like this. I can handle dying, but I cannot handle the pain of getting there. The pain is unbearable, so I have to do something to relieve it." That tearing pain returned to my stomach as she talked. I wanted to take this away from her more than I'd ever wanted anything, but I couldn't. All I could do was tell her I loved her, would pray for her, would always think of her.

We reminisced about fun times in tiny bathrooms, staying overnight with Mama during her final hospital night and how we had talked all night long as Mama lay there. We talked of good times and difficult ones, but I know she knew I loved her— that's what mattered.

Before leaving town, I told her what I'd told Roman—I wouldn't return for her funeral. The time to visit was now. She understood, as Roman had.

While visiting Carol and browsing the hospital gift shop, I found two porcelain dolls. One looked like Bertha in her youth —beautiful, with dark brown hair and milky complexion. I bought my Bertha doll. I also found one with red hair and a gingham dress, small and pretty— My Carol Doll.

Peace cannot be purchased

Once again, I sought to heal the empty space inside my heart.

Once more I thought to cork the hole in me with possessions.

Rather than jewels now on each finger—for how many rings Can one person wear?

I purchased dolls; dolls that reminded me of my sisters in their youth.

Dolls that gave me hope—maybe somewhere, they might have been this beautiful, this peaceful, this happy somewhere, sometime.

The truth I knew peace, beauty, and happiness were not what their lives had measured.

And dolls would never bring back, no matter the cost, lives now treasured and lost.

Carol went home briefly between Bertha's funeral and her final days. I was traveling for work, calling often to stay connected. I felt battle-weary, unable to face more pain.

Working full-time and traveling full time while parenting daughters long-distance, my life was in survival mode. I couldn't even think about going home once more to watch another sister die.

Carol developed a leg infection, and to save her life for even one more day, they amputated it. It didn't matter—I believe it was the day after amputation; she died.

I wasn't there, but I'm told she called her husband and daughters to be with her the night she died. Probably to give her last mothers word of advice.

I'm glad they were all there together that night. I'm sure it must have been a very difficult night for her and her family. No matter if you are "expecting" it, watching someone you love die is horrible. I'm also equally sure it was good for her for them to be there with her and talking with her. That's what matters in those last moments that you are surrounded by people who love you.

Carol's Goodbye

The damage done, her body tired, and her heart sore—She died that night.

Her legacy was her life of unselfish giving and contagious laughter. It was the steady, everyday love she lived without ever realizing how extraordinary she was.

She loved in quiet ways—showing up, helping, caring, doing what needed to be done even when she was sick or exhausted.

She never saw her own worth, but the rest of us did.

We benefited from her giving nature, often unknowingly taking it for granted until she was gone.

Her body was tired, her body worn down, but her heart kept giving. That was who she was.

This was her true legacy: a love so constant and unselfish that we once thought it ordinary—only now understanding how rare it really was.

What does a person say if you know you are dying at any moment? I wonder as a mother, do you try to get in all those last words of advice to your children? No matter their age, mothers are always mothers and our children are always our children so if other mothers are anything like me, we are always giving advice whether our children want it or not. How does one decide what you want to say on your deathbed? Is it all those last things that you want them to remember, and you want them to know about life because you won't be there to tell them anymore.

I like to think she was at peace at her death, and I truly hope that is the case, but I don't know. I hope I'm at peace when my own time comes but again, I'm not sure that will happen. I'm not very accepting of death as our end now. Time may change that.

Carol died forty-two days after Bertha. Her older sister had preceded her by only a short time—maybe that's how their lives had always been, the older sister leading the younger. Carol was only 50 years old when she died. Much too young and much too young for the suffering she endured.

She was gone. I'd talked with her the night she died, not knowing she was dying or having her party. As it happened, I'd called to check in, to say those same words one more time: "I love you."

Right or wrong, I'd decided I could not attend one more viewing of a family member's body. I could not—or would not—fly home for another funeral, knowing one more sister was gone.

Carol was gone, and another hole formed inside me. I wonder when the holes in me will be bigger than me.

CHAPTER 11
THE PATRIARCH DIES

My oldest brother was named after Daddy—Roman Jr— but all I ever called him was Jr. He appointed himself patriarch after Daddy died, the one who thought he should rule us all and I'm very sure that didn't go over well with the older sisters. He was only 14 years old when Daddy died. That is very young to suddenly be the man of the house, and I'm sure expected to work in the field and act like a man would.

My whole life I have looked at my brothers and sisters as older and probably judged them as if they were older. Jr was 10 years older than I but at age 14 certainly not ready to handle adult responsibilities. He got married at 18 and had his first son at 18 and again certainly not ready for adult responsibilities. I am ashamed to say it's taken me all these years to really look at what age my sisters and brothers were when they took on heavy responsibilities and to truly appreciate how young they were and for how well they did for their ages. They were all still teens when they took on wives and husbands and kids so of course, they had rough times and didn't always do everything just right and didn't aways treat their spouses or kids as well as they could have. They were literally still kids themselves.

Until now I've never seen or understood or been able to reconcile the men and women I knew who were loving, kind, funny, great providers, and who unselfishly gave of themselves and worked hard for their families with the ones I saw when I was young. Understanding what their ages were, has given me a whole new respect and love for them all that I so wish I could tell them about now.

My grandchildren are great but at age 17 and 18 are not the least bit ready to take on a household and kids and marriage but all my brothers and sisters did. I have a completely new respect and love for them now understanding this.

Junior was wild in his youth; with an uncontrollable temper he unleashed on his wife and children in his very young adulthood. However, he had first the responsibilities of our farm at age 14 and then a new wife and son at age 18 so his youth was just that, he was an 18-year-old who had not had a dad around to help him grow and had to do it all on his own. So, while I did know him to be hard on his young family he was still more a kid than an adult himself. And his life would not have been easy. I was too young to know how he got into upholstery work or how he learned the trade I know that he set out on his own at an early age and had his own business. Again, without any real education. I have no idea if he finished high school or not but he certainly didn't have business training. Yet he did the work, did the sales, did everything in his business and I know they had some lean times, but I also know they made quite good money and didn't seem to want for much. His work included upholstery recovering car seats, home furniture and not even sure what else.

I probably knew him the least as a young boy/ man but got to know him better from my visits home and he and his wife made a visit out to see us when I was married to my first husband. About ten years separated us, and he married young. When Mama decided to sell the farm, he took it hard, but he wasn't around to help much. Already married or close to it, he couldn't change the sale. He would only have been 25 when I left the south and got married. I lived there a couple of times after that but for no more than a year or so at a time and I was caught up in my own family drama during those times.

He and his wife had 5 children, 3 boys and 2 girls. One of the girls had a birth defect problem and died when she was 3. I'm not sure of all the health details but I know it was a devastating time for Jr and his wife Gaynell. He would have been only 32 years old at the time of her death.

The trip he and his wife made out to Washington to see us was a great time. They were amazed at the trees and all the green and purchased small trees and flowers to take back with them on the flight home. I can't remember how they accomplished that since they were flying and these were not tiny trees. Jr always had jangling keys in his pockets and at the airport he tried to go through security and got taken aside because he had things in his pockets. I will always remember how he stood there with his hands outstretched and them running the handheld machine on his body with him embarrassed but still laughing. He had a great sense of humor.

He and Gaston fought constantly in those early years after Daddy died—I'm not sure about what, just typical sibling battles. However, they were 14 and 13 so they were boys who both thought they needed to protect their mama and take care of the farm. What I remember most about Junior was his nail-biting—he'd bite them down until they bled and his infectious laugh and fun stories he would tell. As adults he and Gaston lived close to each other, and they were forever playing jokes on the other one. These jokes would be major things like going to the other's house at night and banging drums or metal to scare the devil out of the other. It seemed the jokes they played on each other were relentless and each one had to one up the other.

I would not have wanted to be a part of any of the jokes but to listen to him tell the stories they were wonderfully hilarious, and he was so fun to watch and listen to. I can still see him at Mama's kitchen table: eating, talking, smoking, and gnawing his nails to the quick. I loved him dearly and enjoyed every time we had together. He and his wife would come over to Mama's when I would visit to see me, but they were night people and would come over at 10 or 11 at night. It was so much fun around that big kitchen table. Mama would have the food out early in the day and sisters would come over to see us and talk and have fun. Then she would put the food away for a bit and we might take a rest and then Jr and Gaynell would come over and probably some of the sisters as the table was always full of people. What fun times with Jr telling stories and all of us laughing.

While we girls endured our own hell—no daddy to protect us from uncles and cousins who saw fit to "get to know us"—the boys faced their own torment. The uncles and cousins in our family would tease the boys mercilessly. They played practical jokes on them and roughed them up all in the name of "fun"

The boys grew up rough and hard, with tempers to match. This was the temperament they carried into marriage—my brothers expected their wives to obey orders without question. Junior was hard on his wife and children for years, as he grew up and sowed his wild oats. He didn't treat them well in some areas, but he loved them all dearly and was always proud of them. He worked hard to provide for them to give them a good life. When I first wrote this book I didn't really think about the ages of my brothers and sisters and now as I rewrite some of my stories, I realize how young Jr was when he got married. Later in life as an actual adult he mellowed and was a great husband and father. They were together until he died and I know they had hard times, but they stayed together and loved each other to the end.

I remember there were times when I was at home and young and they would come over to visit with Mama. I think some of them would start to play cards or some sort of games and they would do that for long periods of time. Gaynell would be trying to take care of the kids, and she would be ready to go home but Jr was into the games they were playing. Gaynell would ask him and ask him, and he would keep putting her off, till she just said that is enough and put the kids in the car and left him sitting there. I have no clue how old they were or how old I was but the look on his face was priceless. I can still remember it and laugh about it. I don't remember how he got home or if it happened more than once. But Gaynell would take only so much from him and then she would lay down the law.

So, while they were rough with their wives the wives didn't sit and take it they argued and fought back and put them in their place many times.

Unlike my sisters, who developed Type 1 diabetes early in life, Junior was diagnosed with Type 2 at forty-one. We'd all believed that if you escaped the dreaded disease before forty, you were safe. We were wrong.

Junior could take pills instead of injections, and we hoped he could control his diabetes and live a long life. Type 2 is supposedly more manageable with diet and exercise—maybe that's true without other complications. But Junior also had heart problems requiring open-heart surgery.

He was a chain smoker, starting as a young boy, never able to break the habit. After his first surgery, doctors warned that continued smoking would kill him. He tried briefly, then returned to cigarettes. Five years later, he needed a second surgery. After that, his decline accelerated.

Between heart disease and diabetes, he became homebound— unable to sleep, enduring constant pain and suffering. He was miserable in his final years. He died at fifty-eight, leaving his loving wife Gaynell and four children. Gaynell who was and is like a sister to me was always right by his side and took excellent care of him throughout their marriage. Not to say she was walked on and used however because she had a fire in her and she made sure she got him in line when he needed it. But like many women in the south, she did have to endure a lot she should not have. She has always been one of my favorite people in this life.

When I'd attended Bertha's funeral, Junior had said he understood my decision not to return for his funeral. That night at his house after the service, we'd talked about many things. I told my brothers how watching them mistreat their wives had affected me—how the beatings they delivered to their wives made me certain I'd never marry a Southern man. Now at this age I wish I could go back and show them some understanding of the fact that they were so young and still trying to become men and had probably taken on too much. Not that it is ever ok to hurt anyone, but I understand it more now.

Being Southern had nothing to do with it, but in my mind it did. In my mind, the South meant men being "head of household"—in charge, entitled to beat wives for any infraction, free to have affairs with impunity. I wanted as far away as possible from the South that was my reality—to leave and stay gone.

I never wanted to marry a Southern man who'd expect me to wait on him and accept whatever he dished out. Of course, that kind of thinking had led to my marriage at fourteen—with all the consequences that brought.

I did love going home and sitting around Mama's kitchen table, listening to Junior's stories. He'd sit there gnawing his fingernails, telling us about pranks he'd pulled, laughing until we were all laughing with him for hours. And we were always eating, of course.

I was in California on assignment when I got the call that Junior had been hospitalized. He died shortly after. There wouldn't have been time to reach him even if I had tried.

There was always the dilemma of when to go and how long to stay. My family had been so consistently sick, so perpetually close to death, that I never knew when to visit.

I felt resigned to pain, to death, to the smell and feel of death, shame, and suffering. I didn't know how to heal, so this became one more death whose pain I shoved inside. Inside, I could pretend it didn't exist—that I didn't feel the sorrow, pain, or loss.

Occasionally the pain raised its ugly head, but I pushed it down again. Time has helped somewhat; it's gotten easier, but it's always a part of me.

Periodically I've tried walking away from writing this book, but like an unrelenting boss, it calls me back. The writing summons me, waking me up as if my family's story belongs to it, not me. My body remembers things, pushing and pulling fragments of information up to my brain, urging them to emerge.

So here I am again, finishing my family's story.

Writing Calls

It's been a while—life in the way—but here I am again with much to say.

The South still calls but duty bawls: much to do here this day, leave the writing and let it wait.

Another day, one more sunset, one or two sunrises to go. The fear and the pain drive me away once again.

Urgently now the writing looks to escape, wins the battle, demands release, heats my inner self and takes the lead.

So now here I am again to let it out, to have its say.

CHAPTER 12
RUTH'S WINTER

I started writing this book last year, and when I began, Ruth was alive. I questioned her about details of both our lives as the story unfolded. As the year progressed, so did her illness. She died September 18, 2004.

Death had given us a six-year reprieve before arriving to claim one more sister. Ruth's official cause of death was "failure to thrive"—a new term for me, though it hardly captures the horror of watching your sister go through physical and emotional hell and then die.

But before we get to all that, as I sit writing this, I think of how passionate she was about everything she did. Too much so sometimes but she certainly gave her all to whatever she did. One time when she and I lived not far from each other in Oregon she came over to ride horses with me. She didn't really know how to ride as she hadn't been around horses much, but she jumped on and away we went. We did fine on the way out but on the way home as horses will, they decided to speed up to get home faster to their food. We were on a paved road, and they had shoes on but normally I would never run the horses on a paved road. Well, they took off like a "bat out of hell" as the saying goes and while I the "horsewoman" was scared Ruth just pushed her horse on and they flew at a full gallop the rest of the way home. How we made it home safely I will never know but we did with Ruth laughing all the way and me in almost a panic.

On another day when I was pregnant with my last daughter I went to her home and we decided to cut her grass but we didn't have a lawn mower nor a tool of any kind except scissors so we took scissors out to the grass and there we were when her husband came home me very big and pregnant and her laughing as we cut the grass with scissors.

It was during their stay in Oregon that Mike and I divorced so having them around was a big help that I needed. Ruth would watch my daughters for me often during that time and she and her husband Ray would teach them songs and games as Ray played his guitar. It was both fun and hard for the girls as they had lots of rules for them, but I was very grateful for their help. Ray told me during this time as he watched my life that I had two speeds full bore ahead and totally down, nothing in between. I think he was right, and I can't say I have changed too much.

Ruth was the third sister in our family, counting both from top down and bottom up. Funny—I never realized that before. Not sure if it has meaning or just is.

She married at sixteen and had one daughter. Her husband Jimmy was big, tall, dark, with a temper to match his height— but Ruth had a temper that nearly matched his. They were terrible together. He beat her repeatedly before she finally left, never to return. I know of one hospitalization with a broken nose and black eyes—I don't think it was the only time.

The years following her divorce were filled with turmoil. She drank heavily and "ran around" a lot. I believe Mama cared for Ruth's daughter as much as Ruth did during this period.

After a few years, she met Ray on the west coast. They lived together, then married after a couple of years. About five years into their marriage, Ruth became a Christian—and never one for half measures, she became fanatical in her beliefs. This didn't lessen her love for God, but it made her judgmental of others who didn't share her convictions. Many felt she pushed too hard for their comfort.

In spring 1989, Ruth and Ray felt God calling them back to North Carolina. They bought a manufactured home and placed it beside Mama's to help care for her. At the time, I didn't think much about their return, but they became invaluable to our sick and dying.

They'd been back less than a year when Mama died. Then Ruth devoted herself to helping Berline, then Bertha, then Carol. While I escaped some pain by maintaining distance, she was present for each death, giving freely of her time. Though sometimes frustrating family members with her pushy beliefs, Ruth was there, helping each one, never considering herself.

I don't think she ever allowed herself to mourn their deaths—I believe she carried their pain in her body when she died. I've come to believe our bodies house all old memories somewhere in our cells, heart, and brain. Our bodies remember pain and hurt, storing everything inside.

I'm not sure how we end pain or truly heal, but I believe that by not allowing yourself to feel memories and pain, they grow bigger inside until they consume your body entirely. This is what I believe happened to Ruth.

She had rheumatoid arthritis, but people live many years with this disease. Ruth was diagnosed around 1989 and died in 2004 —fifteen years.

I believe she would have felt guilty not continuing to carry their pain. Last year, after months of midnight writing, I realized I felt guilty for having more than my siblings—as if being happy while they suffered was wrong. When this intuitive thought struck me about myself, weeks later came the knowledge that Ruth had never allowed her body to release our family's pain. Because this came intuitively and spontaneously, I believe it's true.

Fear of Success

I'm afraid of success—I just had an intuitive pop:

It's not failure I've fled, but success is my dread, I just realized in my head.

For love of my family who are dead, I don't deserve to live without dread.

So this then is my fear: I might find happiness and cheer when you've had so much to endure.

It is your pain that resides in me, causes me not to be free!

Where is my right to freedom of flight when your wings were clipped and you could not soar?

Your pain beyond control resides in my soul, causes me not to be whole— freedom and success it stole.

If success is my bed, what does that say about me—your life lived without gain?

That I had no care of you, no regard for the pain that you go through?

What gives me the right to have peace at night when your body is full of fright?

How can I think of gain and fanciful things while you are so full of pain?

How can I allow myself success if loyalty to you I possess?

I didn't know this was part of me—the fear that I would be alright and being alright feels like it betrays you!

Ruth and Ray lived in North Carolina twelve years—long enough to watch Mama, three sisters, and a brother die. Ruth's arthritis worsened progressively. She could only move from chair to chair with a walker, spending most time in a wheelchair.

She tried many natural remedies for pain and disease progression. Deathly afraid of doctors and distrusting them, her medical visits were minimal. During those twelve years, new drugs were released that might have slowed her disease, but since she avoided doctors, she remained unaware of them. We'll never know if she might have lived longer with less pain had she sought treatment.

With immediate family either dead or living elsewhere, Ruth and Ray decided to return west. Three of us lived out here now, so they wanted to move closer to the remaining family. Fall 2000, they drove out and bought a small house south of Olympia, Washington.

They tried positioning themselves between the three of us—me, youngest sister Roma, and younger brother James. Unfortunately, by getting "in between," they weren't close to any one of us, so visits and help were limited. Other than occasional visits and phone calls, I didn't see them much until Ruth's health deteriorated significantly.

On one infrequent visit, I was shocked to see both Ruth and Ray had lost tremendous weight, especially Ruth. She looked like a Holocaust victim or one of those starved women from third-world countries on television. Her eyes were so sunken they looked like holes in her face—mere skin stretched over protruding bones.

I tried hiding my shock with casual conversation, but I'm not sure I succeeded. We talked, and I realized she was deeply depressed and seemed to want to die. Her life had become isolated and lonely, but in her painful, crippled body, going out was impossible. All her time was spent just surviving, and Ray's time was spent helping her meet daily needs.

We discussed her weight, and she promised to eat and regain strength. When Cliff and I left that day, I cried most of the way home. She was living such a horrible, painful existence—once again, watching someone I loved with terminal illness threatened to destroy me.

The next few months were torture for all of us—Ruth, Ray, James, Roma, and me. Many trips to Ruth's followed: visiting, helping, interviewing in-home healthcare workers. Days and nights became one nightmare after another.

On one visit to help, I realized how dire things were. Though Ruth's body was failing, her mind remained sharp as a tack—she knew every medication and timing. Her mind was bright, but her body couldn't keep pace, so she constantly thought of ways to feel better or rearrange the house for easier living. I'm sure she didn't realize she could have kept two or three people busy constantly!

Like the rest of our family, her mind kept going regardless of how tired her body was. I was up every five minutes doing something for her and was exhausted after just hours. That's when I knew she needed full-time care—more than any one person could provide. No wonder Ray was so sick and tired—he'd been doing this for five years.

When Ruth needed the bathroom, I helped her up and walked behind to prevent falls. When I helped her pull down her pants, I became immediately sick seeing her back and tailbone—

nothing but skin over bones. Her backbone showed in knots down her spine, her tailbone protruding with no fat or muscle covering. I could see her entire skeletal frame through skin so thin and porous it seemed nonexistent.

I felt horrified—sick with revulsion and sick with sorrow. I tried hiding my face so Ruth wouldn't see my shock.

We joked about spending most of our lives trying to lose weight and how she didn't need to worry about that now. She laughed, saying she needed some of that weight back. I tried keeping things light as my stomach threatened to expel everything inside.

We made our way back to her bed—me trailing behind as she inched along, one sliding, shuffling step after another. No more than three feet, but it felt like forever.

She asked me to help reapply a hand and arm bandage meant to relieve pressure and pain. As I rewrapped her arm, my fingernail lightly brushed her skin. She jumped, saying it hurt, and she'd probably need tissue for blood. I thought she was overreacting—my finger barely touched her. I looked down and grabbed tissue just in time to catch blood rolling down her arm from the wound I'd caused.

I gaped at her arm, hardly believing what I saw. Even knowing how thin she was, I had no idea how easily she could be hurt. One more horror in what I'd begun thinking of as the house of horrors. I'd been there only hours and already felt I'd go mad with the sight and smell of death in motion.

Help me find my way

I come today to you to say: Help me to find my way.

I'm lost in the sea of life like a boat drifting on ocean waves.

Rising high, dipping low, it carries me wherever it chooses.

I have no sail, no power—drifting, riding with ocean waves.

Riding high just to drop, rolling with one wave followed by another.

Lord, lift me up, fill me to the brim with your power.

Hold me up till the tide rolls me in, that I might stand on land again.

I spent the night there with Ruth, and Cliff and I were awake most of it. Ray took antidepressants and stayed in his room all night and most of the next day. He seemed in the throes of a nervous breakdown—no wonder, with the strain of watching Ruth's pain and her constant needs. There was no time for him to even walk outside—she was so frail she could fall anytime.

I'd been sure we could bring them to stay with us, but it quickly became impossible. She needed a hospital bed and numerous other equipment just to function, including a special toilet because she couldn't reach the bathroom. Moving her on short notice was impossible, and Ray was too sick to make the trip.

Ruth needed one to two people at her side twenty-four hours daily. First, there was no money to fund this; second, they lived so remotely we couldn't find helpers.

James arrived the next night, and we discussed options. I hadn't realized he'd been coming for months, trying to help and encouraging them to get healthcare workers. They didn't want strangers in the house, didn't want to spend their little money, and I believe Ruth didn't want to admit needing that level of care.

We stayed through that night, but the next day had to go home. James and his daughters stayed to help through another night, but then Ruth and Ray were alone again.

Disasters started happening one after another. Ruth was determined to have her infected bottom teeth pulled despite our attempts to dissuade her. She was insistent, so she went in for extraction.

They had to anesthetize her for the procedure, but when time came to wake her, they couldn't. She had to be hospitalized, put on oxygen, and kept overnight. They wanted to keep her longer, but she refused. The doctor told her she was malnourished and needed care, but it didn't matter—Ruth checked herself out and had James pick her up.

We were all angry because at least in the hospital she'd be cared for. It didn't matter—she went home again with no one to care for her, leaving us worrying about what would happen.

Ruth went on and off medication. When she took enough to ease pain, she'd fall asleep mid-conversation, no matter what she was doing, even going to the bathroom or doing any normal daily activities. At night she woke every forty minutes to use the bathroom.

After returning from the hospital the first time, she had caregivers most of the time. Finding workers in her area who she liked was a constant battle. Within days of coming home, one night caregiver called saying they couldn't make it. Ruth took the call but didn't tell Ray, thinking she could handle it and wanting him to rest.

Ruth's sharp mind couldn't imagine her body wasn't keeping up, and she desperately wanted to stay home and let Ray sleep. She got up to go to bed and somehow fell. Her leg practically burst open, and Ray found her in a pool of blood on the floor. They had to call an ambulance.

CHAPTER 13
ON HER TERMS

Cliff and I had planned a trip to eastern Washington to explore relocation possibilities, but I knew Ruth would be terrified in the hospital, so I headed down to see her. James had been with her when they bandaged her leg—they couldn't stitch it due to her thinness and condition. James had returned home for work, leaving her alone.

The five-hour drive to the hospital felt endless. When I walked into her room, her face crumpled with relief.

"I didn't think you were coming," she managed to rasp, fear etched on her face.

"Of course I would come," I answered, my insides crumbling.

Her nurse spoke gently: "Now don't cry, she's here now."

"She's not going to cry," I quickly replied. If Ruth cried, she'd choke and couldn't breathe, so I closed off my feelings so that I could help her. I hugged her and focused on getting her to lie down and relax.

We talked, and I told her I'd been angry when she went home before because we wanted her properly cared for. She apologized but said she'd rather die than be in a hospital or nursing home. I let it be.

I rubbed her head and laid fingers across her brow to relieve pain. As I rubbed her head that night, she started dozing. Before sleep, she whispered:

"Don't be mad at me for going home. I'll stay as long as I can."

My heart broke, tears springing to my eyes as I choked out, "I won't be mad at you. Do whatever you have to do."

I waited until she slept, then drove the five hours home that night. I cried most of the way. Dear God, it was so hard watching her pain and suffering.

Ruth went home the following day—she couldn't stand the hospital any longer. I desperately tried getting full-time home help but couldn't find enough people. Then I tried convincing Ruth to consider assisted living.

Ray wanted her to have full-time help; she insisted she didn't need it. I yelled at her on the phone one day, told her she was being selfish, that Ray couldn't care for her and we wanted her properly cared for.

She stood firm, and all I felt was sorry for adding to her suffering by trying to force something she clearly couldn't do. For her, going to hospital, nursing home, or assisted living was like dying

—she'd have preferred death to any of those. She seemed out of options. We got her as much help as possible, knowing the money wouldn't last, but we had to honor her wishes and help her die at home if it came to that.

We had a short reprieve, then got a call from their neighbor that Ray had threatened suicide. Paramedics were called, and after settling things down, they took Ray to the veteran's hospital in Portland for treatment and rest, where he stayed about a week.

Little by little, this crisis ended. Ray was released, Ruth agreed to full-time help, but finding good help remained difficult given their remote location. The struggle continued, as did worry about money running out. At least there was brief quietness where we could all catch our breath.

This lull lasted about three weeks. James, Roma, and I were exhausted from worrying and trying to help, which included hours on the phone with each other. We let things drift temporarily.

I believe Ruth decided to die sometime in this last year—I'm not sure when. I also believe she then decided she didn't want to die and tried everything to regain weight and health, but it was far too late.

Ruths decision

It might be truth and it might be lie, but I believe my sister decided to die.

She reached the conclusion her life lacked function—this is not allusion; she arrived at a junction.

Believing her life's work complete, her desire to be with God so sweet, body failing, her mind in a blood heap.

With determination and vision, she reached the decision to end the division of body, mind, and spirit.

She purposed the time and she chose the place. Always full of grace, she ended her race.

The next time I saw Ruth was the day of my ex-father-in-law's funeral. My daughter Tammy called to say her grandfather had died and the funeral was Saturday, September fourth. I hadn't seen my ex-husband or his family for years, but his father had been the closest thing to a father I'd ever had. My love for him and my mother-in-law was, and still is, very strong.

I called my other daughters, saying we all needed to attend. Beverly flew out from Colorado on Friday for Saturday's funeral. I called Ruth and spoke with Ray instead—this had happened two or three times recently, and I was worried. We'd rarely gone more than a few days without talking since they'd moved west. If Ruth wasn't coming to the phone, something was wrong.

Ray said she was depressed and bedridden, so we'd stop by the next day. He thought that was good.

That night I went to bed before Cliff, unusual in our house. I was asleep, or in some sleep state, when he entered the room. As he prepared for bed, I began screaming at him relentlessly. I clearly saw the death angel standing by my bed, telling me he'd come to take my father-in-law. It was incredibly real—as if a person stood beside my bed, this death angel announcing he was taking Dad.

Cliff turned on the lights and shook me awake, then held me until I could sleep again.

This chapter on Ruth has been, and is, so hard to write. Maybe because it's so soon after her death, maybe because I'm tired of feeling pain. In my head I'm screaming: Lord, don't you know how hard this is? What do you want from me? Why do I need to write this? Who is it for, and who cares if I write it or not? Is writing about all this pain ever going to make it stop? I don't want to feel it anymore. I just want it to go away! Dear God, I do not know how to heal!

We went to the funeral, then stopped to see Ruth on the way home. She was bedridden now, pretty much constantly, unable to get up even for the bathroom. I sat by her bed, and we talked briefly. She was very weak, and I knew by looking at her she didn't have long.

"Some of these people hurt me," she whispered, referring to caregivers. "I'm afraid," she continued in a barely audible voice.

As tears started falling again, I answered softly, "It's okay to be afraid, Ruth."

She seemed to consider this. I wasn't sure what we were discussing exactly—did she think she wasn't getting good care? Did she feel mistreated by workers? Was she afraid to let go and die? I tried comforting her but wasn't sure what to say or do. I felt as though a hammer had slammed my skull and was pounding me into the ground. There seems no way up from this hammer that keeps slamming me down each time I struggle to rise.

I tried lightening her mood by talking about old times. I reminded her of visiting my house and riding one of my horses down our long driveway onto the road, galloping up and down while I was terrified. We laughed so hard about that, and she said:

"You didn't know, but I was so scared all I could do was hold onto the horse and let him do what he wanted."

As we talked, I saw the look of love pass between her and Ray, and I knew that regardless of how hard these times had been, they both loved each other deeply.

I called Roma on the way home, and she decided to go stay with Ruth. We agreed I'd drive down Monday and pick her up in Tacoma to take her to Ruth's.

That night, tired from the funeral and Ruth's visit, I went to bed before Cliff again. The scene from the night before repeated itself, but this time when I saw the death angel, I knew he'd come for Ruth. I partially awoke to see the "death angel" there to get Ruth. I was screaming Ruth's name again followed by "No! No! No!"

Cliff woke me and held me until I calmed down. But now I knew without doubt that my sister wouldn't be much longer in this world. I had been pre-warned.

During this past summer, as Ruth went from one agony to another, James, Roma, and I spoke often about how much we could do to help her. We discussed what we could do while remaining sane ourselves, and we spoke of things we could leave undone without feeling guilty when she died.

But as much as we talked, and as sure as I was that I was doing all I could, I remain guilty. Is this always how it is when someone close dies? Do you always feel guilty? It seems no matter how much I think I won't, I still do, and I still know there was more I could do—more times I could have called, more visits, more help in her agonizing path to death. Dear God, there is always the guilt of the "should haves." Will they never end? Will I ever feel like what I did was enough for my sisters, my Mama? Will I ever be satisfied with what I gave, and not wish I had done more?

Ruth

I watch you, my beloved sister, die slowly suffering, agonizing pain, losing your dignity and privacy in your own home, at the mercy of others to meet your simplest needs.

Dying released you from the ghastliness your world had become. I was relieved to see you go.

Now I question myself; Am I relieved for you or me? Or is it both?

I can't watch this pain anymore! I want this pain to be gone!

I want you to go, leave! Don't be here anymore—but then who's this thought for? You or me? Me or you?

Though my head says you, my heart knows the truth, my body feels the shame that I'm so selfish—

I did not want to watch your misery anymore. Watching brings so much pain to me.

Did I let you down and ask that you go too soon for me?

While my mind tries to fool me, my heart knows the truth— truth brings remorse and guilt that I could be so self-centered as to be glad that I do not have to view your pain and suffering anymore.

Did I let you down and ask that you go too soon for me?

I drove Roma to Ruth's house on Monday, beginning the last two weeks Ruth would live. Roma stayed to help her and Ray cope with everything: pain, medication, strangers in their home.

Ruth's hospice nurse told her that when she got pain under control, she would probably die. She explained that many times, it's the pain and fighting that pain that keeps people alive. She said when and if Ruth wanted, she could go into the hospice center and let them give medication to control pain, but when pain was controlled, she'd probably go to sleep and not wake up. She also offered medication at home to relieve pain if Ruth chose this route.

I found it amazing that just by fighting pain, it would keep you alive, though when I thought more, I realized how this could be true. When I'm fighting anything, my body cannot relax and stays in fight mode, but when I stop fighting and allow things to happen, my body relaxes and moves with life's flow—and in this case, death.

I spent one night there with Ruth that week. She'd asked James, Roma, and me to come because she wanted to talk. She explained what the nurse had said and asked what we thought about going into the hospice facility. She told us she wanted things easy for Ray—she didn't want him thinking of their home as just the place she died, and she talked about his depression the last few months. She said no matter what she did, she couldn't seem to help him.

As she lay in bed with the three of us around her, she tried helping us understand her decisions and asking our blessings— or at least our understanding.

"If I could do anything, if I had some purpose," Ruth spoke quietly. "The nurse says I can go into hospice, and they'll give me medication, and when that happens, then I just won't wake up," she continued.

The three of us sat and listened, unsure what to say. How do you say it's okay to allow yourself to die? How do you say you've suffered enough pain here?

"I have tried and tried to make Ray happy and help him get beyond his depression," Ruth said, "and I just can't seem to help him. I think it would be best for him if I don't die here."

Ruth, always in control, always thinking of the big picture, continued speaking softly—as if discussing a movie, they might see rather than her impending death.

James, Roma, and I finally started talking to let her know we understood and supported her, whatever she decided.

"Ray isn't going to feel any differently about this house whether you die in it or not," James told her. "You both have lived in this house, and your memories will be here no matter what you do."

"Ruth, we are behind you, whatever you decide to do," we all chimed in.

Who would have ever thought the three of us would be sitting at our sister's bedside giving her permission to die?

Ruth had made her decision but had enough love and respect for us to want us to know why, and to help us understand and support her. There were many times Ruth had made me angry because she was so strong-minded and strong-willed, but now she just made me proud to be her sister.

As the next few days unfolded, it was clear that God must have planned them. It was as if He and Ruth orchestrated her death to bring us all closer together and to know without doubt that He had a hand in the whole process. Putting it in words will never bring justice to the events, nor will mere words show the love and hand of God as He unfolded this last chapter of Ruth's life, but I hope you'll get some idea, even if slight.

Ruth started talking about a party—first it was going to be a rededication of her and Ray's wedding vows, then as talk contin-ued, it moved to a going-away party. She was quite excited about planning this party and gave Roma the songs she wanted sung and what she wanted to eat. At day's end, James and I headed to our respective homes to wait for the next phase. Roma had decided to stay to help, and regardless of her own sickness, she was intent on being there to help however she could.

Our older brother Gaston had told Ruth if she gained weight and made it back to at least 100 pounds, he would fly out from Maryland to see her. He'd been trying to give her incentive for gaining weight, as she really wanted to see him.

Gaston had always stayed as far away as possible from our family's dying process. He found it very difficult to be around and had told Mama he would not go to another family member's funeral again. I knew Ruth wanted him to come desperately, but I honestly didn't think he would. I wanted to try persuading him anyway, so I called to tell him that if he wanted to see her, he needed to come out. I didn't know how long she had, so I couldn't tell him that—just that we knew it wouldn't be long.

"I called Gaston to tell him what's happening with you," I told Ruth that day.

"What did he say?" she asked.

"Well, I spoke with his wife Bobbie, and she said they couldn't get tickets until the last weekend in September," I relayed.

"Well then, that's the time for my party. Tell him I will try to wait," Ruth spoke almost cheerfully. If anyone had heard our conversation, they would have thought we were planning a tea party, not a death scene.

I hung up and called Gaston back to tell him she said she'd try to wait. I didn't want to alarm them because I really didn't know how long Ruth had, and I still wasn't sure Gaston would really come, so I just told them what I knew—that Ruth would try to wait, and I truly didn't know how long she had.

Only hours later, Bobbie called back to say they'd be flying out in a few days. They'd fly on Wednesday, and we could drive down Thursday morning to see Ruth. James, Roma, and I were surprised that Gaston was coming—shocked is more correct. Ruth was elated, and I cried when I heard how happy she sounded.

Gaston and Bobbie flew in the following Wednesday, then we all drove down to Ruth's on Thursday. She was very happy to see him and spent considerable time telling him the same things she'd told us, then asked if he had anything to say. Gaston told her he didn't, just that he loved her. She was satisfied with that.

We'd all been afraid of how Gaston would react to seeing her condition. Though he was very broken up, he stayed with her and spent the day, except for occasional smoke breaks. He'd surprised us all by showing up, and I found myself getting to know my brother for the first time in my life.

We spent the day with Ruth and Ray, then headed to the hotel Thursday night. James and his wife Sandy and daughters went home that night, and Roma stayed with Ruth.

The next morning, Gaston, Bobbie, Cliff, and I went to Walmart to pick up snacks for Ruth's that day. We'd picked up some things and were in the parking lot when Gaston asked if we thought we should take her a birthday cake. He was tentative about it, but when he asked, I thought: What a perfect idea!

We headed back into Walmart to get the cake. We found some nice ones but couldn't decide what colors to get, so we called

Ruth to ask her favorite color. She told us yellow, then blue, so we found her a pretty birthday cake with yellow and blue roses.

When we arrived back at Ruth's, James wasn't there, even though he'd called saying he was leaving hours before. We anxiously awaited as Gaston wanted to give Ruth her cake. It took quite a while for James to arrive—we were beginning to worry when he finally drove in.

He had several boxes with him and brought them into what had become the smoking and break room in the garage. He called Roma and me out to our "break room" and told us: "I decided that I was never going to buy my sisters dolls again, so I got them all today, so I don't have to think about it anymore."

He handed Roma a doll that looked just like her with blonde hair and nice pearl and rosy cheeks. Then he handed me two dolls with light blue dresses and long curly hair.

"I didn't get to buy Berline her doll, so I bought hers now for you," he said to me. Tears slid down my cheeks as I hugged him and thanked him for the dolls.

Next, we lit the candles on Ruth's cake, and all walked in together to give it to her, along with her doll and a stuffed animal that James's daughters had brought. Ruth had gotten one of her caregivers to paint her toenails, so to add to her gaiety, I gave her a purple ribbon for her hair.

Her little face, surprised and radiant, lit up like a Christmas tree with thousands of lights all sparkly and bright. She was like a little girl who'd never gotten a birthday present or had a birthday party—she was so excited she could hardly contain herself. We captured the surprise on her face on video, but I doubt I'll ever forget how happy she looked.

What's amazing is that no one had any of this planned. Gaston felt foolish, he told us later, but he kept thinking about that cake; and James had headed over from home and made a snap decision to find those porcelain dolls. So, each brother and sister had, in their own way, contributed to a wonderful birthday for our sister Ruth. The fact that it wasn't even her birthday played no part in our party at all. A birthday party is truly in the heart anyway.

Roma was quickly proving herself the best nurse Ruth could have, taking the lead role in all Ruth's care. Roma, the little sister who'd always had so many medical problems herself, and who'd assumed her "role" in all family functions in the past, was now the leader and expert we all looked to for advice and help.

I had written a poem for Ruth, and when I had the chance, I read it to her with Ray by her side.

Ruth

She lay in her bed where pain has tread, beads of sweat upon her brow, purple ribbons laced within her auburn hair, purple toenails to brighten her stay.

Lips moist like morning dew, eyes as a clear blue sky, her face serene, no wrinkles do appear, porcelain skin a rosy hue.

Peaceful in this new day as her life blood ebbs and flows away, she knows her time is near and watchful as a deer, she waits her Lord to hear.

She dies as she's lived— in control, on her terms.

Courageous woman scared little girl, strong willed, sharp creative mind.

Hardly a speck of gray weaves its ragged way into her wavy auburn mane. She said no, and it dared not come.

No one could tame her free spirit to the end.

Mind alive, mind of steel, but some things in life not meant to control, not meant to win.

A time to live, a time to die, a time to let go of all. A time to fight, a time to cry, a time to rest, a time to mourn.

Body worn, body tired, struggle and strife no more.

She hears God's call, clouds and storms to shore. So much pain one to bear, but now surrenders all as quietly, gives her last requests.

Her mind at rest, her fear is gone, her fighting done and work complete.

Spirit runs, breaks free, laughter tickling through the trees to God she moves in peaceful glee.

She lays there, her face aglow with peace as she let's go!

James's daughters made our old-time Southern favorite, chicken and pastry, and brought it over to Ruth's for dinner. Ruth ate the chicken and pastry and cake and whatever else she wanted that night. We all thought she was going to make herself sick since she hadn't been eating much.

"Ruth, honey, you better not eat too much, or you'll be sick," Roma told her, watching like a mother hen.

"Roma, what does it matter? Just let her eat it," Bobbie spoke up.

What did it matter indeed, I thought, since we knew Ruth had only hours left to live—what did it really matter?

"I just don't want her to be sick," Roma answered, "but you're right. If she gets sick, then I'll just clean her up."

Ruth ate as much as she wanted—quite a variety of food too— but for some reason, she didn't get sick from the mixture or amount. Her diet had consisted of crackers and protein drinks for months, and not much of those either, so it was a miracle indeed that she didn't get sick.

The day was Friday, and Ruth had made tentative arrangements to go into the hospice facility on Sunday to be put on medication and then be allowed to die. We knew she didn't want to go to the facility—her desire was to die at home, but she made arrangements anyway, just in case. We all told her that when the time came, she didn't have to go—she could just stay home. She was torn between not wanting Ray to see her die and not wanting to leave home. She'd fought for years to stay home, so it was hard for me to imagine her going into the hospice facility. We all knew that wasn't what she wanted.

That night we all gathered in her bedroom, bringing in chairs so we could sit around her bed with her as the center of attention. We talked some about our youth and some about what was happening now. Ruth was the true Southern hostess at her party.

Since writing was very new to me, I surprised myself by asking Ruth if she'd like me to read everyone the poem I'd written for her, and she said yes. The night just unfolded—I read her poem with everyone present, and it felt like my gift to her. A gift of praise and recognition for who she was.

I think we all cried some when I read it, and then we each had an opportunity to say to Ruth and to each other what each meant to the other. It was one of the most beautiful family times we'd ever had. Over the last few years, Ruth had wanted us all to get together, reminding each of us more than once how important it was to see each other before it was too late, and now on her deathbed, she had accomplished what no one else had accomplished in years.

I told Ruth how proud I was of her, and each of us in turn told her how much we loved her and each other.

God and Ruth had choreographed an event that will forever be stamped in our memories—a night full of love, praise, and openness for and about each brother and sister. We were a family unit that stood together and said, regardless of hurt in the past and hurt now, we were family, and we were a strong unit that death could not and would not break.

It seemed that God and Ruth had planned a role for each of us. We had each, without talking about what we were doing, just done the right thing at the right time. I wish I had more words to convey the magic of that day and night, to tell you how not of this earth it was—how heavenly we all knew this to be. Cliff said there was something or someone working there that weekend; there had to be. Cliff is not a superstitious man, so when he said that it was further confirmation to me of the miracles we had witnessed.

The night ended, and even though Cliff and I had planned to go home that night, we didn't—instead we stayed so we could see Ruth in the morning.

The next morning, Roma met us when we got to Ruth's, and we could tell she was upset. She told us that Ruth had had a hard night and that they'd thought she was gone at one point. Gaston and I went in to see her, and both of us broke into tears—she was writhing on the bed and clearly out of her head. We watched with our hearts in our throats as her head moved from side to side and her eyes glazed over.

I rubbed her brow and told her we were there, and she seemed to recognize us. We stayed in the room beside her as long as we could tolerate the pain, then left to get fresh air. Roma, our Roma, stayed with her and gave her pain medication. I wonder if Roma will ever really know how much we all appreciated her that week and weekend. She was the strongest I have ever known her to be and clearly proved to herself and us that she was beautiful inside and out.

When Gaston and I went outside, we were both pretty broken up. James hugged me and laughed a short laugh.

"Don't worry, Sugar, I have seen her like this a hundred times.

You see her and you're just sure she's going to die, and then the next time you see her, she's up and at it again."

I remember thinking, I'm not sure this time, James—I'm just not sure. Then a short time later, when Roma came out to tell us that Ruth wanted us to come in and visit, the thought crossed my mind that maybe he was right after all.

The Final Songs

We went in to see her, and she had rallied—she was ready for us all to visit again. James brought out his guitar and played a few songs, and we all sang some of the old hymns we knew, with Ruth chiming in right along with us. James had written his own melody to the song "The Way That He Loves" to sing for Ruth, so when there was a lull and some had gone out to the "gathering place," he sang it for her.

The group had put the monitor out in the gathering place so even when one took a break, they could still hear what was going on in Ruth's bedroom. The song was beautiful, and you could see in Ruth's eyes how much she liked it—her face glowed with peace and contentment.

After singing Ruth's song to her, James asked Ray if he would like to play, and Ray started playing and singing all the old songs he and Ruth had sung together. Ruth sang at the top of her lungs in a bright clear voice, and you couldn't hear any sounds of sadness or pain there. As Ray played and sang and Ruth sang along with him, there was that look of love that passed between them, so astonishingly beautiful, that I was once again struck by the thought that, no matter what, their love for each other had remained very strong.

After we sang for a while, we could see that Ruth was getting tired, so we wound things down to let her rest. Once again, the staggering pain gripped her, and her body started shaking. I was standing next to her, and she sort of laughed up at me and said, "I can't seem to stop my head from shaking."

Once more I rubbed her brow, telling her to just relax. She asked me to scratch the back of her head, so I did, feeling crushing pain in my chest as I felt how small her head was. It felt like touching a skeleton. I continued to rub her brow, speaking softly and gently, hoping to help her relax, telling her that her work here was done now, that she could just rest, she didn't need to worry anymore.

Then as she lay there, I said, "Ruth, when you get to Heaven, will you send me some kind of sign so I'll know you're really there?"

"Okay," she smiled her answer.

Gaston, Bobbie, James, Cliff, and I got ready to go. Gaston and Bobbie were flying out the next day from Seattle, so our plans were to drive back into town that afternoon and be ready to take them to the airport the next day. It was pouring rain as we prepared to leave. We each went in to say goodbye to Ruth. Even though she was very tired and her eyes had glazed over again, she seemed to know each of us as we said goodbye.

It took us about three hours to get home that day as traffic was somewhat lighter than usual. We had not been home long when

Roma called to say that Ruth had died. She was pretty upset and said that Ruth had stopped breathing—she was pretty sure she had died but was not totally sure.

I had answered the phone and was in some slight shock—even though we had seen her dying, maybe you never really believe it IS going to happen. It seemed that when Ruth had finished her party with us and with visiting, she had just decided: now it was time to go. It was truly like she had orchestrated the entire event to the exact time that she wanted it. Ruth was only 56 when she died.

I didn't know what to tell Roma, and since James was in the background telling me to relay to her some of the things she needed to do, I put him on the phone. He'd been through this kind of thing before because his wife's sister had died in their house, so he knew the formalities to follow. He spent time talking with Roma, telling her what to do, while Gaston and I hugged each other and listened in some shock and silence.

Afterwards we talked about the timing of her death, and of how Ruth had managed this weekend, of how not of this earth it had been, and then, exhausted, we went to bed.

The next morning, Roma called to tell us they were planning a service on Tuesday. We were all surprised, because we felt that our service had been Friday night. We didn't see how anyone could improve on that, and to be honest, Gaston and I were more the ones who simply didn't want to go to a service. It just felt like more than we could handle.

Gaston told me again that he had said he would never go to another service after Mama's, and I just didn't want to endure more pain. So, Gaston decided he would go home as scheduled, and I said I wasn't going to the service either.

So, the day progressed, and we took Gaston and Bobbie to the airport and said a tearful goodbye. This had been the first time I'd had an opportunity to really get to know Gaston and Bobbie, and I'd enjoyed them so much, I was sad for all the lost years between us. I had run so far and so fast all those years, and so had Gaston, both of us in our own way, so there had been no time to get to know each other as adults. I knew then just how much I had missed by running away and not making the effort to stay in touch and see each other more often. It is always so easy to look back at your mistakes, but very difficult to know at the time what is the right thing to do when you are set on just surviving life.

I spent Monday just recuperating; my plans were still not to attend the service. Ruth's daughter was flying in from out of town that night, and Roma would pick her up.

Tuesday morning came, and as I sat and had my coffee, Cliff asked me what I was going to do. I was a little surprised because I thought I had made my decision. Cliff said he thought we should go, so I called James to see what he thought, talk it over with him. We discussed it, and I decided to just let Cliff decide. If he thought we should go, then we would go. When I told him it was his decision, Cliff said, "Then we're going," so with no time to spare I jumped in the shower and got ready to go.

Ruth's body had been cremated, and her service was to be at the church in the little town of Ryderwood where she and Ray had lived. We started our drive, and as I sat thinking about the last week and the last few days of Ruth's life, I decided to write another poem as we hurried down for this final chapter of her life.

Family Tradition

In our family of death and dying we've had this tradition of mourning and crying, viewing the body of our loved one lying in wait to reach that Golden Gate.

Now sister Ruth made other plans. Knowing her time was near, she called: sisters and brothers, come here.

Come to my side, let's do some singing. It's time to break this old family tradition.

And unknown to us all, she orchestrated a family ball!

She had sister Roma attending her every need, brother James singing and bringing her dolls, while brother Gaston bought a birthday cake when he had sworn: "I'll never again watch a loved one die."

Sister Earline wrote of times gone by and gently rubbed her brow.

She and God at work brought out the best in us as we had our old-time family reunion.

"Come in to visit with me, talk to me, sing to me, have a little glee. Scratch my head, rub my feet, let's have something good to eat!"

She talked of her life and spoke of her death—she was looking forward to her rest as she gave her last requests.

Asked each of us: "Do you have something to say?"

We talked of family gone on before, expressed our love and pride to be the sister or the brother of the other.

We spoke of all the fun we'd had and all the pain we'd had to bear, but when the night was done, we knew the other a little more and we were closer as sisters and brothers!

Husband Ray strummed his guitar, playing and singing Praise to God!

Our Ruth rallied and sung in perfect tune!

Then her last task on earth complete, she smiled and moved to Jesus' feet.

Roma and her husband Roy planned the service and had everything in place when we got there. Roy asked me to read the poem I had written for Ruth. Roy played the guitar and led us in some hymns, and Roma gave each of Ruth's caregivers an opportunity to say something and then gave them each a small gift to show our appreciation for all the work they had done for Ruth.

I then read the first poem I had written for Ruth and then the second one that I'd written on the way down that day. Ruth had wanted us to sing "How Far is Heaven," so Roma, Roy, James, Sandy, and I sang it without music. This old song felt like it had been a part of me forever, for as long as I could remember, and here we were singing it once more.

I thought about how different this small service was compared with what it would have been had we been back in North Carolina where all the extended family would have attended. The church that day had a very good crowd, more than I would have expected since they hadn't lived in the community that long, but it was still very small compared to what it would have been. It didn't matter—it was what Ruth would have wanted, and it was very special, and I was very glad that I had attended.

On the way home later that day, Cliff told me that I had done a beautiful job in reading the poems, and I realized that him saying that meant as much to me as an Oscar would.

So, one more sister was gone, and we were left to mourn and wonder how long we would have until one more brother or sister left us. While four is a good number of brothers and sisters, when you start out with nine, then four is no longer a good number.

I feel scared and battle worn and am not sure which turn to take in my life these days. The need to finish this story has pushed me on, and so now, coming to an end, I'm not sure how to proceed from here. I still don't know for sure if this has been healing for me—I've spent many hours crying as I've written this story of our family, and the pain of their loss is still there. I'm old enough and have lived through enough deaths to know that time will ease the pain, but I don't know if it ever goes away. Somehow, I think not.

One last tidbit: if you remember, I had asked Ruth to show me a sign if indeed she made it to Heaven to prove to me there was a Heaven. I had said it half-jokingly, but in my heart, I knew I really did want a sign. No matter what, it seems the doubts and questions remain, and it's like I just want God to step down and say, "Yes, I absolutely do exist, there absolutely is a Heaven."

In the days after Ruth's death and service, I waited and waited. It had been about a week, and I found myself disappointed, like the atheist who says, "Ha ha, I told you God was not real."

Then that night a program came on television on a channel I wouldn't normally watch. Usually I'd just flip by, but this night, something stopped me. I started listening to what they were saying—it was a program about "near death experiences," and whether they were real, and whether some form of life after death actually exists.

Cliff happened by, and we both sat mesmerized by what we were hearing. The program featured medical doctors, PhDs, etc., in many scientific areas of research talking about the research they'd done. There were many highly educated people doing research in a variety of ways who said, "Yes, there is some sort of life after death, place, or experience."

Hearing that the left-brained, thinking world was saying, "Yes, there is life after death," added validity to the idea, for no matter how much I try to tell myself that things in life do not have to be proven to be real, there is, and maybe always will be, that smidgen of doubt.

My spirits seemed to lift after seeing that program, and while it could be coincidence, I took this as a message to me from Ruth and God to answer my question.

CHAPTER 14

WE ARE THE MESSAGE

The pain of losing my family members crashed into me during menopause like a dam finally bursting. Everything I'd stuffed down, pushed aside, or simply survived came flooding back with a vengeance. Those were brutal years—it felt as if I had no choice but to review my life and face the grief that I had buried inside my body like stones.

I was drowning in emotion most of the time, crying at the smallest things. One afternoon, sitting in the Safeway parking lot with tears streaming down my face, I turned to Cliff and said, "I don't know what's wrong with me. It's taking every ounce of energy I have just to get through each day."

He reached over and took my hand, but I could see the worry in his eyes. How do you explain to someone that you feel like you're dissolving from the inside out?

Another day, my youngest daughter came home to find me sobbing while mixing batter for her birthday cake. When she wrapped her arms around me and asked what was wrong, the only thought in my head was that I was dying.

"I feel like I'm dying," I whispered against her shoulder, the cake ingredients forgotten on the counter.

The deaths of my family members sat on my shoulders like a twenty-pound bag of potatoes that I carried everywhere I went. I kept wondering what my life had been about, what my purpose was, and what was the point of striving so hard to succeed if we were all just going to die anyway. It took everything I had to keep going, to keep myself from shattering into a million pieces.

During this dark period, I spent as much time as I could outdoors with my horses or working in the yard, seeking something I couldn't name. Then came that autumn day that changed everything.

I was kneeling in my flower bed, pulling dead marigolds and withered petunias, my hands black with soil. The October air was crisp against my face, carrying the earthy smell of decomposing leaves. As I worked, yanking the brown, brittle stems from the earth, something shifted in my understanding.

The parallel hit me like lightning.

We must die to make room for those coming after us.

I sat back on my heels, dirt-covered hands resting on my thighs, and suddenly saw it all so clearly. If these flowers didn't die back in fall and winter, there would be no space for new life in spring. The soil would be overcrowded, choked with old growth, and the new plants would wither from lack of room to flourish.

All at once, it made perfect sense. To everything there is a season. The plants live, some producing beautiful blooms that bring joy through sight and fragrance. Then autumn arrives, and the flowers must surrender to make room for the next generation of life. Each has their own message, their own purpose, their own light to offer the world.

We must make room for all those who come after us—the children and grandchildren who arrive with their own gifts, their own dreams, their own reasons for being here. Our purpose is to shine our light, whatever that light may be, for our allotted season. Then we step aside, lovingly, to give them space to bloom.

I wish the flowers could tell me where we go from here. I wish they could speak and lay to rest my doubts about Heaven, but they remain beautifully silent. Some days I believe our souls live on in some magnificent other place. Other days I wonder if we simply go to sleep, never to think or dream or love again.

But just as love is a choice, I think belief in life after death is a decision. I choose to believe there is continuation in some form when our bodies fail. I choose hope over despair, faith over emptiness.

And for now, I know I have work to finish. When my time comes—my autumn or winter—I hope to go willingly and gracefully, the way the rest of my family has gone before me.

Today, my siblings and I stand at different points in our own seasons. I have two brothers and one sister remaining, each carrying forward the family legacy in their own way.

My brother Gaston has some heart trouble but seems to have it under control for now. He represents the determination that runs through our bloodline—the refusal to surrender without a fight.

James stays healthy despite the normal aches that come with living. He embodies the generous spirit that our parents modeled, always ready to help someone in need.

My sister Roma battles Type I diabetes, the same disease that claimed so many of our sisters. She's had it since age ten—almost forty years now—and there have been countless times we thought we'd lose her. But Roma chose early to become an expert on her own survival. She studied everything about her condition, changed her diet, and took control in ways that continue to amaze me.

After watching Mama, then Berline, Bertha, and Carol die from this same disease, Roma went through her own period of living like there was no tomorrow. Unlike the rest of us, though, she already carried the enemy inside her body. She lived through her own version of hell, knowing she was seeing a preview of her possible future.

Now she's remarried after her divorce and seems genuinely happy. Every day she remains healthy feels like a gift—to her and to all of us who love her.

I'm 54 years old as I write this, and I've been healthy most of my life. But recently, the family shadows have begun touching me too. High cholesterol, high blood pressure, and just this month, elevated blood sugar levels that mark me as borderline diabetic.

When the doctor delivered that news, I cried for two days. I'm not sure why—I'm older now than any of my siblings who died from this disease. I'm healthier than Mama was at this age. But still I wept, feeling that familiar hole opening inside me, fear rippling through my chest like cold water.

I'm terrified of this disease. Terrified of enduring the living death I watched my family suffer. Afraid there won't be time to accomplish everything I want to do before my season ends. And maybe, underneath it all, I'm afraid that after I'm gone, there will be no one left to remember that I lived at all.

My Reckoning

April day, sun shining, breeze blowing My heart weeping Fog clouds my brain.

Warm salty wet drops seeping Down my face like rain.

The lady in white gave me the news in a hurry, almost as if a passing remark: Your bad cholesterol continues to rise to the roof and high blood pressure is here to boot.

Now, by the way, your last three-month blood glucose leaves little to boast about—I'm afraid that diabetes has come to roost.

Diabetes, our family thorn, heart disease, our family crown, Left me alone but here today, Here to stay I'd say.

This diagnosis forced me to confront the deeper questions I'd been wrestling with. What had my whole life been about? This constant feeling of trying to catch up to something lost, something I could never quite reach.

Writing this book about my family became my way of looking back to understand who I am and why I've made the choices I've made. It became about healing the hurt of losing the people I love most. It became about pulling my fears out of the dark hole where I'd buried them and bringing them into the light, hoping that exposure would rob them of some of their power over me.

Most of all, it became about paying tribute to my Daddy, Mama, sisters, and brothers—creating something permanent so they will always be remembered and honored for who they were.

The writing inside me has pushed and pulled and begged for release. I wake at night hearing its voice. It greets me with my morning coffee and whispers to me as I fall asleep. This story has taken on a life of its own and will not rest until it's told.

Many times, this past year I've asked myself: Is there any uplifting message here? What's the purpose of writing this? Is it just a release of my pain, and if so, will that help anyone else?

My friend Elaine asked me when I got past all the feelings from my youth—the shame and pain. When she said that, I thought to myself, *you know, I'm not sure I have gotten over it.* Maybe writing this story is that getting over it, but I honestly don't know.

Then this morning, as I lay trying to sleep while words spun through my head, it hit me like revelation:

I'm the message. My Mama was the message. My Daddy, my sisters and brothers—we are the entire message.

We have been real survivors. We haven't needed a television show to prove it—each day has been survival for us. We have overcome sometimes-impossible odds, and in doing so, we've left messages for those who come after us.

My Daddy, who died praying for courage to return to his hell in the mental institution so he could get better, left us a message of love and dedication. His legacy includes entrepreneurship, fearlessness about hard work, faith in God, and proof that you can rise above how you were raised.

But he also left warnings: about the destruction that comes from overwork, about the need to rest both physically and mentally, about questioning what medical professionals tell you and finding help to understand before you submit entirely. Your life may depend on it.

My Mama gave us her strength, determination, love, and sharp mind. She kept us together when letting us go would have made her life easier. She showed us love and commitment by caring for us all those years, working two jobs while raising her children.

She left us a legacy of singing on the way to work, of maintaining faith even when circumstances looked hopeless. She cried, but she also laughed and survived, growing more loving with age rather than bitter. She was brilliant, and I never met anyone who didn't adore our Mama.

Her legacy includes resourcefulness—finding ways to make ends meet when there wasn't nearly enough. It includes unselfishness—eating the chicken backs while telling us she preferred them, when the truth was, she was giving us the best parts and eating only after her children were fed. She was love and faithfulness embodied, showing us how to fall and get back up.

She also taught us to hide some feelings to avoid hurting her. While her message of love, honor, and commitment rings clear to me as an adult, as a child I could have used more hugs and hearing "I love you" spoken aloud. Children don't always under-stand the sacrifices their mothers make. But Mama taught us to take what we have and make the best of it, and to never fear hard work in pursuit of our dreams.

My brother Roman may have been wild in his youth, but he raised five children and demonstrated true faith, strength, and love, leaving them that precious legacy. A born entrepreneur, he built and ran a successful upholstery business.

Like our parents, he passed on faith in God and strong family loyalty. He had that same work ethic Mama and Daddy modeled. Roman gave us the joy of sitting around talking about old times and new ones, showing us the value of the kitchen table for keeping love and communication flowing. He proved that while youth may bring an almost out-of-control race with life, a man's true character always shows itself—and inside Roman was pure love and commitment to family and God.

My brother Gaston had an even harder path because he was among the oldest when Daddy died. With no formal education, he started and ran a highly successful electrical business, then expanded into cable—creating something he could pass on to his children and grandchildren.

When I asked him about sales for his company, he said simply, "I taught myself how to do it." This man never lost his sense of humor, remained loving and kind, and had no one to help him through his youth except himself. Neither of my brothers finished high school, let alone college, but that didn't stop them. They learned what they needed and created successful lives, passing on remarkable legacies simply by living with integrity.

My sister Bertha always made me feel loved and special. With her, I could do no wrong, and I always knew she was proud of me. Only after her death did I discover she made all my siblings feel the same way.

She left a legacy of love, caring, laughter, and deep faith in God. But she also left a warning about the harm that comes from holding feelings inside, about how life can spiral out of control when you can't express emotions or get help because everything is moving too fast and too hard.

Above all, Bertha was the embodiment of demonstrative love— hugging us, telling us she loved us, making us feel like the most important people on earth, laughing and crying with us. She was an exceptional cook, always ready to prepare our favorite meals. She taught us hospitality regardless of how much money you might have. Many times, she couldn't afford to make us elaborate meals, but she and Joe always welcomed us like royalty in their home.

Carol left us laughter—at herself and at life. She could laugh at a moment's notice and have you laughing with her. She taught us how important it is to appreciate and value who you are, to give love to yourself first so you can bring that value to others. She showed us the importance of recognizing our strengths while acknowledging our weaknesses.

Carol demonstrated the enduring bond between mother and daughter that runs deep and strong. She left us the message of finding love and fun even in the darkest times, of getting up and moving forward even when sick and weary, of never giving up, of hard work and commitment.

In her later years, when she finally had time for creativity, she made beautiful lamps—showing us our family's artistic gifts in female form. She was friendship, love, and laughter. Like the others, she carried quiet, firm faith in God. She taught us how crucial it is to handle conflicts as they happen and to resolve issues with those we love before our time on earth ends.

Both Bertha and Carol were shy, yet each had wonderful senses of humor and could laugh at themselves as easily as anything else. Both maintained deep faith regardless of circumstances. To say they "just lived their lives" sounds simple, but living your life when it's full of pain and misery requires tremendous strength and fortitude.

Berline, my twin sister, left a legacy of courage in the face of inhuman trials. She had determination to exhaust every possibility and fight for wellness against impossible odds. She showed us how to maintain hospitality and elegance even when physical and emotional pain reaches horrific levels.

She left us that fighting spirit—to battle if there's a chance to win, and to graciously surrender when there's no hope left. She was courage, love, graciousness, elegance, determination, strength, and faith all wrapped into one extraordinary person.

Berline left me with knowledge of connection—of knowing things about each other that can only be understood at an instinctual level. She gave me unwavering belief in higher communication. She taught me that while I may not always understand how messages arrive, I should trust them and know that God has many ways to let us communicate with each other and with Him. Above all, she left us a legacy of faith and hope in God during good times and especially during those lonely, painful moments.

My sister Ruth left us profound messages about life and death. She chose when to die and how to die. She showed us her incredible intellectual and emotional strength. In her death, she demonstrated how partnership with God allows you to accomplish almost anything.

Ruth got the very best from others, and most importantly, she demonstrated faith and love for God even as she lay dying. She left us a legacy of being happy and content to die and join her God, showing her faith by peacefully surrendering herself to Him. She may have been the strongest woman I've ever known, and she directed even her final hours on earth.

Both Berline and Ruth endured years of pain and misery but consistently demonstrated grace, love, and strength. They maintained their faith in God despite their circumstances, touching many lives and leaving great legacies of love, grace, strength, and finally, acceptance. Both were exceptionally bright with quick minds and wit, strong personalities balanced by great capacity for love.

My brother James, not so little anymore, is smart, funny, and talented. As a child, he would give his last dime to someone in need; as an adult, he continues giving to others without regard for himself. He's raised four exceptionally talented children who all share deep faith in God.

Like his older brothers, James never finished high school but started his own electrical business and achieved the level of success he chose. His priorities have always been clear family has mattered more to him than becoming wealthy by material standards alone.

My youngest sister Roma is a success story just by being alive today. She has endured decades with diabetes, and I've never heard her utter an angry word about having the disease. I'm sure she was angry at ten, but as a young woman, she read, researched, and figured out how to care for herself, living with this condition most of her life.

The only anger I've heard from Roma is frustration at others' lack of understanding—people who think if she just took better care of herself, she wouldn't have problems. Roma has taken better care of herself than anyone I know. Type I diabetes kills, maims, and tortures, and while self-care matters, it doesn't heal.

She watched our sisters die horrible deaths, knowing she could easily follow the same path, yet she's rarely shown bitterness. She's been determined to live as healthily as possible, showing remarkable discipline in eating and health habits. She's been loving and supportive—we couldn't have managed Ruth's illness without her. Roma set aside her own health needs to care for Ruth during those final weeks.

Roma is extremely intelligent, has worked for political campaigns and doctors, and I believe that without diabetes, she could have run for office or become an outstanding nurse. She is a success story in her own right.

And then there's me. I have survived and even thrived. I have four beautiful daughters and ten grandchildren. Each is successful in their own way—intelligent, smart, funny, and excellent parents themselves. They all finished high school and continue learning and growing both formally and informally. I couldn't leave a better legacy than them.

We are the message—the message of hope, of life, of each generation doing better. Not just financially better, but better with emotions, better as mothers and fathers and human beings.

Each of us has demonstrated great faith in God. While we dare to question Him, our questioning comes from a lifetime of relying on Him for our very survival. We don't always understand, and though our pain sometimes threatens to overwhelm us, we love Him with fierce devotion.

We have each survived hardships in our own way. Like our Mama and Daddy, we have endured. We've lost battles, but we've been fighters, survivors, and optimists about life and what it offers. Mama and Daddy did leave us a magnificent legacy after all.

Until writing this, I didn't realize that one of our strongest family traditions has been—and continues to be—laughter at life and ourselves and love for each other along with the will to survive and thrive.

I want to take this opportunity to say thank you, Mama, and thank you, Daddy, for who you were and what you passed on to us. Thank you for staying with us when it would have been easier to let us go. Thank you for love and strength shown in countless ways, not always appreciated at the time. I love you both and hope to see you in Heaven.

I want to say how proud I am to be the sister of each of my brothers and sisters. You are and were truly the best message and the best legacy for your children, just by being who you are and were. I love each of you, and as I've written about our trials, I've come to know and appreciate you in entirely new ways. Thank you for being part of my life. Until we meet again!

Story Ends

As I end my story It's the Christmas season and I've heard it said things happen for a reason.

This year I laugh with family members dear. Cry for those no longer here.

As my spirit lingers on loved ones past, I can't help but add this last:

Hold close the ones you cherish. Remember the lines and wrinkles in each face

Whisper your love before they perish. Earth may need some space.

For as winter turns to May and spring and summer need more room.

Death and darkness may come your way and leave you filled with gloom.

But, just remember, flowers Will once again bloom.

EPILOGUE

Twenty Years Later - 2025

I originally finished this book in 2005, believing then that I had captured our complete family story. But life, as it does, continued to write itself.

Gaston died June 22, 2011, of cancer at age 69. Roma died January 8th, 2019, at age 65, from diabetes and heart-related issues—the same family demons that claimed so many others.

Now, my brother James at age 72 and I at age 75 are all who remain of our immediate family. We both have outlived all our siblings. This is something to be celebrated and mourned in equal measure.

I have not felt the pull to add more to this memoir until now. Perhaps because the story feels complete—not because death completed it, but because the message was always there, waiting to be recognized. **We were always the message.** Each loss only made that truth clearer, each survival only made it stronger.

The seasons continue. The garden still teaches. And the message—Our message—lives on in the children and grandchildren who carry our light forward into whatever seasons await them.

APPENDIX

References
Insulin coma treatment

Fink, M., Shaw, R., Gross, G., and F. S. Coleman. "Comparative study of chlorpromazine and insulin coma in the therapy of psychosis." Journal of the American Medical Association. 1958; 166:1846-50.

Rinkel, M., and H. E. Himwich. Insulin Treatment in Psychiatry. New York: Philosophical Library, 1959.

Sakel, M. The Pharmacological Shock Treatment of Schizophrenia. New York: Nervous and Mental Disease Publishing Co., 1938; translated by J. Wortis.

Electroconvulsive Therapy (ECT)

Fink, M. Electroshock: Restoring the Mind. New York: Oxford University Press, 1999.

"Electroshock Revisited." American Scientist. 2000; 88: 162-7.

"Meduna and the origins of convulsive therapy." American Journal of Psychiatry. 1984; 141:1034-1041.

Fink, M., Green, M., and R. L. Kahn. "Experimental studies of the electroshock process." Diseases of the Nervous System. 1958; 19: 113-118.

The following is information I obtained from a paper prepared for the U.S. Department of Health and Human Services Substance Abuse and Mental Health Services Administration Center for Mental Health Services in 1998 by Research-Able, Inc.

"*In 1938, Ugo Cerletti, an Italian neuropsychiatrist, applied electric shock to the brain of a person with a serious psychiatric illness. In the 1940's and 1950's, ECT was used mainly for persons with severe mental illness residing in large mental institutions (mainly State hospitals). The 1985 Report of the National Institute of Mental Health (NIMH) Consensus Development Conference on ECT (4) described these early efforts:*

"*ECT was used for a variety of disorders, frequently in high doses and for long periods. Many of these efforts proved ineffective, and some even harmful.*

Moreover, the use of ECT as a means of managing unruly patients, for whom other treatments were not then available, contributed to a perception of ECT as an instrument of behavioral control for patients in institutions for chronically mentally ill individuals."

In the early years, many fractures and even a number of deaths were associated with the use of ECT.

It is believed that the largest category of people receiving ECT are elderly, depressed women who are inpatients in general or private psychiatric hospitals. (9) Most States do not require physicians to report ECT use; therefore, annual estimates of the number of patients receiving this treatment are speculative. What scientific data do exist suggest a great deal of regional variation in its use -- more so than for most other medical and surgical procedures. (10)

Administration of ECT

ECT involves the use of controlled electrical currents of one to two seconds in duration that induce a 30-second seizure. Generally, the procedure involves attaching two electrodes to the scalp, one on each side of the head, although physicians sometime place the electrodes on only one side of the head. Often, two or three treatments are given weekly for several weeks. In its early years, ECT was administered to patients without prior medication. Today, however, anesthesia, muscle relaxants, and electroencephalographic (EEG) monitoring during and following treatment, enable the physician to closely check patient reactions.

Douglas G. Cameron (26) of the World Association of Electroshock Survivors, addressing the Public Health Committee of the Texas House of Representatives in an April 1995 public hearing to consider a ban on ECT, captured the strong feelings of many ECT opponents with the following statement:

(ECT is) "An instrument which has injured and destroyed the lives of hundreds and thousands of people since its inception and continues to do so today."

Despite support from Cameron and others, proposed legislation to outlaw ECT was not enacted by the Texas legislature.

Comments contained in a two part series in USA Today (27) typify how some of the popular press view ECT:

"After years of decline, shock therapy is making a dramatic and sometimes deadly comeback, practiced now mostly on depressed elderly women who are largely ignorant of shock's true dangers and misled about shock's real risks."

Peter Breggin, a psychiatrist in private practice, strongly opposes the use of ECT. He characterizes the effects of ECT as "brain injury." (39)

Leonard R. Frank, a writer often cited by ECT opponents, received combined insulin coma-electroshock in early 1962. He charges, "... ECT as routinely used today is as least as harmful overall as it was before changes in the technology of ECT administration were instituted." (40)

Linda Andre, Director of the Consumer Rights Advocacy Group, the Committee for Truth in Psychiatry, states that all ECT involves involuntary treatment. Her organization, whose 500 members have experienced ECT, asserts that all patients receiving ECT are under some form of coercion. They maintain that ECT causes permanent head injury (brain damage). Recently, Andre stated, "Forced shock is the most profound violation of the human spirit imaginable. The use of force is a second injury superimposed upon the damage of the shock itself."

My Experience with ICT

Max Fink, M.D.

William Karliner, M.D.

Dr. Fink was in charge of the insulin coma unit at the Hillside Hospital in Glen Oaks, Queens from 1952 to 1958. He has had an academic career in research and teaching of neuropsychiatry with more than 600 scientific publications and numerous books. The latest is Catatonia: A Clinician's Guide to Diagnosis, Treatment and Neurology (Cambridge University Press, 2002). He is an emeritus professor of Psychiatry and Neurology at the State University of New York at Stony Brook.

In January, 1952 I arrived (as a psychiatric resident-in-training) at Hillside Hospital, a free-standing 180-bed psychiatric hospital at the outskirts of New York City. A specialized 22-bed insulin coma (ICT) and electroconvulsive treatment (ECT) unit served about 50 patients with ICT and 130 with ECT each year. At a time when air-conditioning was expensive and rare, the treatment unit was well lit and air conditioned.

The beds were in two rows. Between the beds were stands for equipment and supplies. The beds and bed-stands were metal coated in white ceramic. The beds were framed with side-rails. Two physicians (sometimes three), four nurses, and an equal number of aides were in attendance. Treatments were given every week-day morning. Nurses wore white, well-starched uniforms, and doctors wore white coats, white shirts, and ties. (Since long ties occasionally became soiled by blood, I took to wearing bow ties -- a habit that persists until today.)

Like McLean Hospital, Hillside Hospital prided itself on the use of psychoanalytic, group, and milieu therapies, and was considered a premier treatment and training center. It had an active and well-regarded residency training program. In 1954, it developed a research department that flourishes to this day. ICT and ECT were the secondary treatments offered patients when they were not amenable to psychotherapy. In the hierarchy of treatments, ICT was the last resort.

What did a patient experience in ICT?

Before Coma

He was awakened at 0600, dressed in cotton shirt with short sleeves, and long drawers. No food was given. Taken to the ICT unit and assigned to a bed.

Temperature, blood pressure, and heart rate were recorded. An intramuscular or (occasionally a subcutaneous) injection of insulin was given (usually in a shoulder or buttock, in rotation). Insulin was withdrawn from a vial with a rubber top. Dosage had been assigned the day before.

Stages of Coma

0630-0715: Pre-comatose.

Patient went gradually to sleep and then to coma. Two forms of coma were recognized, a "wet" and a "dry." In the "wet" form, sweating was profuse and was accompanied by "goose-bumps" in the skin. Salivation increased, so much so that nurses sopped it up with gauze sponges. In the "dry" form, the skin was hot and dry, muscles twitched, in a sequence that began in the face, arms, and then in the legs. These were often small twitches, but from time to time, patients would move and jerk an arm or a leg. Occasionally, a grand mal seizure supervened.

Patients sometimes complained of being chilled, and blankets were usually placed as covers.

While most patients were sedated, some became excited. Restraints were applied (usually a bed sheet folded in quarters and tucked under the mattress).

0715-0745: Stage-1 coma.

Patients no longer responded to voice or to touch. The Babinski test, an abnormal neurological sign, became positive. (The doctor would stroke the outer part of the sole of the foot, from heel to outer two toes, and look at the movement of the big toe. A "normal" movement of the toe is downward. A "positive Babinski sign" is an upward movement of the big toe. This indicates that the "higher" brain functions are impaired.)

0745-0830: Stage-2 and Stage-3 coma.

Breathing became slow and stertorous. Eye movements wandered. The pupillary response to light was still present. Occasional spasms of the main body muscles were seen. Sweating was severe, and temperature rose.

In time, breathing became irregular, pulse rapid, and corneal and pupillary reflexes absent. Deep tendon reflexes were lost (striking knee gets no knee-jerk and shining a light gets no pupillary reaction).

Coma stages were checked every 10 minutes. The time of stage-2 coma was noted. The coma was ended from 30 to 60 minutes later, according to the doctor's prescription.

How was the coma ended?

Administering glucose ended the coma. Most often, a "gavage" tube (a thin rubber tube) was placed through the nose into the stomach. The nurse would then administer between 200 cc. and 300 cc. of 50% glucose solution.

A second method was the intravenous administration of 25 cc to 50 cc of a 10% glucose solution. In both methods, patients would awaken quickly.

What was the patient's experience on awakening?

When a patient became conscious, his responses would be slow, with a thick (drunken) speech. Within 15 minutes, he recognized the nurse and doctor, knew where he was, and asked for breakfast. He was very wet; often the bed was soiled. He was taken to a recovery room, showered, and allowed to dress in ward clothes.

Patients were fed their breakfast either in the treatment room or on the ward. Patients ate avidly. It was commonplace for patients to gain considerable weight during the months of a treatment course.

Recollections of thoughts and anxieties were reduced. Patients became calm, less concerned about delusions and hallucinations (these disappeared in successful treatments), and approached their families in a more friendly manner. Those who had been excited and needed restraints, no longer required them.

Patients spent their days reading, meeting with family, or taking part in the hospital routines. Some patients exhibited a silly laughing or crying, without regard to the immediate experience. Transient neurological signs -- weakness of an extremity or errors in speech (aphasia) -- were common. Memory of the illness and recent public events became less clear, but patients retained good recollections of personal memories.

Recovered patients returned home to their work and to their families. For those who had minimal to moderate relief, further treatment with antipsychotic drugs or ECT was prescribed.

The response of Dr. Nash -- immediate relief with the treatment, return to work after an illness of three years, and then gradual relapse followed a common pattern. For a few lucky patients, the treatment worked well and patients returned to a normal life.

Insulin Coma and Seizures

For insulin coma, Sakel rejected spontaneous grand mal seizures as unwanted, unpleasant, and unnecessary. Seizures did occur during ICT, appearing in the second and third stages of coma, especially during periods of "dry coma." Two schools of thought developed -- those who saw seizures as comparable to the seizures of ECT and therefore favorable for a better outcome, and those who considered seizures as unwanted side-effects.

A spontaneous seizure called for protection of the patient's tongue and mouth, as well as restraint. (Every bed-stand had special tongue guards available to be used when a spontaneous seizure developed. These were wooden tongue depressors, about pen-length, 1/2" wide, covered at one end by gauze, or cotton and gauze, to make a soft mouthguard. Or, rubber-tubing doubled and covered by gauze to make a mouthguard.)

By the 1950s, when a patient in ICT was not improving by 20-25 comas, some physicians augmented ICT by ECT given during the deep coma period, usually at three times a week. (I was taught, and taught others, and still believe, that seizures augmented the benefits of ICT. A spontaneous seizure in ICT was welcomed, and not seen as a bad sign.)

Spontaneous grand mal seizures were infrequent. Muscular twitching, jerking of the extremities, grimacing of the facial muscles, and tortuous twisting movements of the limbs and body were frequent. These occurred in the early stages of the treatment.

How do we understand the mechanism of action of ICT compared to modern treatments for schizophrenia?

The immediate benefits of ICT were increased feelings of well-being and less preoccupation with obsessive thoughts. Weight increased and agitation decreased. For many patients, these benefits were sufficient to allow them to return to home and community. It was unclear then, and remains so today, what mechanism could explain the relief of psychosis.

We do not know why schizophrenia develops in adolescence, why it persists, nor *what is the pathology in the brain that has gone awry. In animal studies, modern medicines affect the brain's neurohumors (such as serotonin, dopamine, and adrenaline). Many scientists believe that aberrations in these systems are the cause of schizophrenia, and see the medicines as redressing hypothesized abnormalities. Such theories are not supported by human research.*

When ECT and ICT were introduced, much academic interest was focused on the brain's electrical activity as measured by the electroencephalogram (developed in 1929). Measurement of the brain's electrical activity during courses of ICT showed dramatic and persistent changes. Amplitudes of the brain rhythms increased, frequencies slowed, and new patterns of spike and slow burst activity appeared. When these brain changes did not develop, the patients did not improve. The benefits of ICT were best assured when the brain's electrical activity changed, and this occurred most often after a prolonged coma. The benefits in ICT were seen to be in developing new (different) brain rhythms of electrical activity that did not encourage psychotic thoughts. Similar observations were made in support of a neurophysiologic theory for ECT.

Different ideas of the mechanisms of action of these treatments come from the roles of the brain's neuroendocrine processes. The body's functions are monitored by chemical substances (hormones) discharged from such specialized glands in the body as the adrenal, thyroid, parathyroid, pituitary, ovary, and testis. These glands are controlled by the brain's neuroendocrine glands, the hypothalamus and the pituitary. The substances are discharged in cyclic fashion, with cycles that are a day, month, and lifelong in duration. The substances determine the diurnal cycles of waking, sleeping, and eating; periodic cycles in sex; and life.

In patients with psychiatric disorders, the hormonal regulations have gone awry. The best example is in major depression where the hypothalamic-pituitary-thyroid-adrenal interactions are grossly abnormal. With effective treatment, as with ECT, these imbalances are normalized. (And when the illness recurs, the imbalances have returned.)

Insulin is a very powerful stimulant of the endocrine and the neuroendocrine systems, as is the coma produced by it. It is probable that insulin coma's benefits may have been achieved by redressing hormonal imbalances, in a fashion similar to that of ECT. (During the ICT era, we did not have the knowledge of neuroendocrine interactions nor the methods of study that we have today.)

Such actions would also explain the benefits achieved when ECT was added to ICT.

Many forms of schizophrenia are identified, labeled as the paranoid, catatonic, hebephrenic, simple, etc. ICT was most effective in patients with the catatonic form, less so with the paranoid, and least with the other forms. Interestingly, the hormonal imbalances are most prominent in patients with catatonic schizophrenia, and less so in the other forms.

These Treatments Today

Today's main treatment of patients with schizophrenia is the prescription of antipsychotic drugs. These offer control of symptoms but rarely offer a cure.

ICT is no longer practiced in the West. Reports of its continued use in the former Soviet Union and in China occasionally appear.

Lobotomy, sometimes called leucotomy or psychosurgery, is occasionally used to relieve patients of agitation and severe obsessive-compulsive rituals -- the patients for which it was first advocated.

ECT is now widely prescribed for the relief of severe psychiatric illnesses. We have learned, to our disappointment, that none of the medications used for the treatment of psychiatric illnesses provide "cures." A percentage of patients quickly become "therapy resistant." The medications fail to control their psychosis, and it is at such times that ECT is widely employed today.

Diabetes

What is diabetes?

Diabetes is a disease in which blood glucose levels are above normal. Most of the food we eat is turned into glucose, or sugar, for our bodies to use for energy. The pancreas, an organ that lies near the stomach, makes a hormone called insulin to help glucose get into the cells of our bodies. When you have diabetes, your body either doesn't make enough insulin or can't use its own insulin as well as it should. This causes sugar to build up in your blood.

Diabetes can cause serious health complications including heart disease, blindness, kidney failure, and lower-extremity amputations. Diabetes is the sixth leading cause of death in the United States.

What are the types of diabetes?

Type 1 diabetes, which was previously called insulin-dependent diabetes mellitus (IDDM) or juvenile-onset diabetes, may account for 5% to 10% of all diagnosed cases of diabetes. **Type 2 diabetes**, which was previously called non-insulin-dependent diabetes mellitus (NIDDM) or adult-onset diabetes, may account for about 90% to 95% of all diagnosed cases of diabetes. **Gestational diabetes** is a type of diabetes that only pregnant women get. If not treated, it can cause problems for mothers and babies. Gestational diabetes develops in 2% to 5% of all pregnancies but usually disappears when a pregnancy is over. **Other specific types of diabetes** resulting from specific genetic syndromes, surgery, drugs, malnutrition, infections, and other illnesses may account for 1% to 2% of all diagnosed cases of diabetes.

What are the risk factors for diabetes?

Risk factors for type 2 diabetes include older age, obesity, family history of diabetes, prior history of gestational diabetes, impaired glucose tolerance, physical inactivity, and race/ethnicity. African Americans, Hispanic/Latino Americans, American Indians, and some Asian Americans and Pacific Islanders are at particularly high risk for type 2 diabetes.

Risk factors are less well defined for type 1 diabetes than for type 2 diabetes, but autoimmune, genetic, and environmental factors are involved in developing this type of diabetes.

Gestational diabetes occurs more frequently in African Americans, Hispanic/Latino Americans, American Indians, and people with a family history of diabetes than in other groups. Obesity is also associated with higher risk. Women who have had gestational diabetes are at increased risk for later developing type 2 diabetes. In some studies, nearly 40% of women with a history of gestational diabetes developed diabetes in the future.

Other specific types of diabetes, which may account for 1% to 2% of all diagnosed cases, result from specific genetic syndromes, surgery, drugs, malnutrition, infections, and other illnesses.

What is the treatment for diabetes?

Healthy eating, physical activity, and insulin injections are the basic therapies for type 1 diabetes. The amount of insulin taken must be balanced with food intake and daily activities. Blood glucose levels must be closely monitored through frequent blood glucose testing.

Healthy eating, physical activity, and blood glucose testing are the basic therapies for type 2 diabetes. In addition, many people with type 2 diabetes require oral medication, insulin, or both to control their blood glucose levels.

People with diabetes must take responsibility for their day-to-day care, and keep blood glucose levels from going too low or too high.

People with diabetes should see a health care provider who will monitor their diabetes control and help them learn to manage their diabetes. In addition, people with diabetes may see endocrinologists, who may specialize in diabetes care; ophthalmologists for eye examinations; podiatrists for routine foot care; and dietitians and diabetes educators who teach the skills needed for daily diabetes management.

The **Diabetes Overview** *fact sheet from the National Diabetes Information Clearinghouse   (http://www.diabetes.niddk.nih.gov/dm/pubs/overview/ index.htm) has additional information.*

What causes type 1 diabetes?

The causes of type 1 diabetes appear to be much different than those for type 2 diabetes, though the exact mechanisms for developing both diseases are unknown. The appearance of type 1 diabetes is suspected to follow exposure to an "environmental trigger," such as an unidentified virus, stimulating an immune attack against the beta cells of the pancreas (that produce insulin) in some genetically predisposed people.

For more information about the immune system, visit these pages from The National Institute of Health's (NIH) National Institute of Allergy and Infectious Diseases Web site:

- The Immune System
- Understanding Autoimmune Diseases

For more information on genetics and disease, visit:

- NIH's Genetics Home Reference
- NIH's Human Genetics and Medical Research online exhibit
- The Centers for Disease Control and Prevention's (CDC) Office of Genomics and Disease Prevention
- NIH's National Center for Biotechnology Information's Human Genome Resources page

Can diabetes be prevented?

A number of studies have shown that regular physical activity can significantly reduce the risk of developing type 2 diabetes. Type 2 diabetes also appears to be associated with obesity.

Researchers are making progress in identifying the exact genetics and "triggers" that predispose some individuals to develop type1 diabetes, but prevention remains elusive.

See the Preventing Diabetes section in the FAQs for more information.

Is there a cure for diabetes?

In response to the growing health burden of diabetes, the diabetes community has three choices: prevent diabetes; cure diabetes; and improve the quality of care of people with diabetes to prevent devastating complications. All three approaches are actively being pursued by the US Department of Health and Human Services.

Both the National Institutes of Health (NIH) and the Centers for Disease Control and Prevention (CDC) are involved in prevention activities. The NIH is involved in research to cure both type 1 and type 2 diabetes, especially type 1. CDC focuses most of its programs on being sure that the proven science is put into daily practice for people with diabetes. The basic idea is that if all the important research and science are not applied meaningfully in the daily lives of people with diabetes, then the research is, in essence, wasted.

Several approaches to "cure" diabetes are being pursued:

- Pancreas transplantation
- Islet cell transplantation (islet cells produce insulin)
- Artificial pancreas development
- Genetic manipulation (fat or muscle cells that don't normally make insulin have a human insulin gene inserted — then these "pseudo" islet cells are transplanted into people with type 1 diabetes).

Each of these approaches still has a lot of challenges, such as preventing immune rejection; finding an adequate number of insulin cells; keeping cells alive; and others. But progress is being made in all areas.

What are some other sources for information on diabetes?

The CDC's National Diabetes Fact Sheet

The National Diabetes Information Clearinghouse

MedlinePlus's Diabetes Tutorial

The following organizations may help in your search for more information on diabetes:

Federal Government Organizations
Department of Veterans Affairs

Internet http://www.va.gov/diabetes/

Health Resources and Services Administration

Internet http://www.hrsa.gov

Indian Health Service

Diabetes Program

5300 Homestead Road NE, Albuquerque, NM 87110

505/248-4182

Internet http://www.ihs.gov/MedicalPrograms/Diabetes/index.asp

National Diabetes Education Program

Internet http://www.cdc.gov/diabetes/ndep/index.htm

The NDEP is a nationwide initiative of the Centers for Disease Control and Prevention (CDC) and the National Institutes of Health (NIH). It is an inclusive, partnership-based program involving many diverse public and private sector partner organizations. The goal of the program is to reduce the morbidity and mortality of diabetes and its complications.

For more information on NDEP, call toll free 1-800-438-5383.

National Institute of Diabetes and Digestive and Kidney Diseases

1 Information Way, Bethesda, MD 20892-3560

800/GET LEVEL (800/438-5383) or 301/654-3327

Internet http://www.niddk.nih.gov/

National Eye Institute (NEI)

Bldg. 31, Room 6A32

31 Center Drive, MSC 2510

Bethesda, MD 20892-2510

301/496-5248 or 800/869-2020 (to order materials)

301/402-1065 (fax)

Internet http://www.nei.nih.gov

Office of Minority Health Resource Center

US Department of Health and Human Services

P.O. Box 37337, Washington, DC 20013-7337

800/444-MHRC (444-6472)

Internet http://www.omhrc.gov/

Non-Federal Government Organizations

Links to non-Federal organizations found at this site are provided solely as a service to our users. These links do not constitute an endorsement of these organizations or their programs by CDC or the Federal Government, and none should be inferred. The CDC is not responsible for the content of the individual organization Web pages found at these links.

American Association of Diabetes Educators

100 West Monroe, 4th Floor, Chicago, IL 60603-1901

800/338-3633 for names of diabetes educators

312/424-2426 to order publications

Internet http://www.aadenet.org*

American Diabetes Association

1701 North Beauregard Street

Alexandria VA 22311

Telephone 703-549-1500

1-800-ADA-ORDER to order publications toll free

1-800-342-2383 (800-DIABETES) for diabetes information

Internet http://www.diabetes.org*

American Dietetic Association

National Center for Nutrition and Dietetics

216 West Jackson Boulevard, Suite 800, Chicago, IL 60606-6995

800/366-1655 Consumer Nutrition Hotline (Spanish speaker available)

800/745-0775

Internet http://www.eatright.org/*

American Heart Association National Center

7272 Greenville Avenue, Dallas, TX 75231

214/373-6300

Internet http://www.americanheart.org/*

American Optometric Association

1505 Prince Street, Alexandria, VA 22314

800/262-3947 or 703/739-9200

Internet http://www.aoanet.org/*

American Podiatric Medical Association

9312 Old Georgetown Road

Bethesda, MD 20814

301/571-9200 or 800/ASK-APMA

301/530-2752 (fax)

Internet http://www.apma.org/*

International Diabetic Athletes Association

1647-B West Bethany Home Road, Phoenix, AZ 85015

800/898-IDAA or 602/433-2113

602/433-9331 (fax)

Juvenile Diabetes Research Foundation

The Diabetes Research Foundation

120 Wall Street, 19th Floor, New York, NY 10005-4001

800/JDF-CURE or 800/223-1138

212/785-9595 (fax)

Internet http://www.jdrf.org*

Medical Eye Care for the Nation's Disadvantaged Senior Citizens

The Foundation of the American Academy of Ophthalmology

P.O. Box 429098, San Francisco, CA 94142-9098

800/222-EYES (222-3937)

National Diabetes Information Clearinghouse

1 Information Way, Bethesda MD 20892-3560

301/654-3327 (phone); 301/907-8906 (fax)

ndic@aerie.com (e-mail)

Internet http://diabetes.niddk.nih.gov/index.htm

ABOUT THE AUTHOR

Jean Starling, the author of *Fallen Leaves: Life, Death, and the Seasons Between*, is a profound survivor whose personal narrative begins in the impoverished South, growing up as one of nine children on a dirt-poor North Carolina tobacco farm. Born as Earline, she reinvented herself as Jean in her youth, seeking acceptance and control over a life marked by poverty, disease, molestation, abuse, and violence. Her childhood ended prematurely when she married at age 14, seeking an escape from a turbulent home life and the lingering stigma that followed her father's premature death due to medical experimentation.

After enduring 18 years in an abusive marriage, Starling made a fierce vow to achieve independence, determined never again to be poor or dependent. She embarked on a rigorous path of self-improvement, quickly earning a bachelor's degree and a Master's in Business Administration (MBA) in rapid succession while raising four daughters and building a consulting career.

The impetus for writing *Fallen Leaves* stemmed from the intense, crushing grief she experienced after losing her father, mother, and five siblings—including her twin sister, Berline—to various illnesses such as Type 1 diabetes and heart disease. She began writing to honor their memories and process the emotional pain, realizing that **"feelings buried alive never die"**. The narrative became an **"unrelenting boss,"** forcing her to confront the deepest traumas of her past.

Starling's memoir is ultimately a powerful testament to the resilience of the human spirit. Her journey culminated in the profound realization that she and her family—with their legacy of faith, hard work, dedication, and survival—**"are the entire message"**. Her story underscores that faith is a **decision** and that wholeness is achieved when two complete people enter a partnership, rather than two halves seeking completion. As of 2025, Jean Starling resides in the Northwest, having outlived all but one of her immediate family members.

www.ingramcontent.com/pod-product-compliance
Lightning Source LLC
Chambersburg PA
CBHW070912130626
46555CB00001B/106